Henry Winthrop Sargent

Skeleton Tours through England, Scotland, Ireland, Wales, Denmark, Norway, Sweden, Russia, Poland and Spain

Henry Winthrop Sargent

Skeleton Tours through England, Scotland, Ireland, Wales, Denmark, Norway, Sweden, Russia, Poland and Spain

ISBN/EAN: 9783744794954

Printed in Europe, USA, Canada, Australia, Japan

Cover: Foto ©Andreas Hilbeck / pixelio.de

More available books at **www.hansebooks.com**

SKELETON TOURS

THROUGH ENGLAND, SCOTLAND, IRELAND, WALES, DENMARK, NORWAY, SWEDEN, RUSSIA, POLAND, AND SPAIN,

WITH

VARIOUS WAYS OF GETTING FROM PLACE TO PLACE, THE TIME OCCUPIED, AND THE COST OF EACH JOURNEY TO A PARTY OF FOUR. WITH SOME OF THE PRINCIPAL THINGS TO SEE, ESPECIALLY COUNTRY HOUSES.

BY

HENRY WINTHROP SARGENT.

NEW YORK:
D. APPLETON AND COMPANY,
90, 92, & 94 GRAND STREET.
1870.

Entered, according to Act of Congress, in the year 1870, by
D. APPLETON & CO.,
in the Clerk's Office of the District Court of the United States for the Southern District of New York.

PREFACE.

The object of the author in publishing these little tours is twofold. One, and the principal, is to answer the universal question of all travellers—"How do you get from one place to another, and how long does it take?" and, secondly, "What does it cost?"

To Americans, who do not shrink from purchasing in London forced peaches at a guinea apiece, the latter question is not usually so important as the former. To most of my countrymen expenditure of time is more disturbing than that of money.

There are plenty of guide-books in the world, and very excellent ones too, which give you every sort of general information when you arrive at a place, and which also give you a general idea of how to get there; but none, that I am aware of, which specify precisely the exact way and time of passing from one place to another. This is especially true of out-of-the-way places—"the nooks and corners of England," and countries comparatively unknown, such as Norway, Sweden, Denmark, Russia, and even Spain. Many travellers would visit these countries, could they have placed before them the exact ways and means of accomplishing these tours, both time and cost. The burden of finding out how to travel in Norway, for instance—how to get there, where to go, what to see, and what money to take—is so great, that impatient or indolent persons give it up in despair, and prefer to follow the old beaten tracks of Italy or Switzerland, or spend the balance of their time and money in Paris. It is to aid this class that these little guides have been published. The author does not pretend that they are the best routes that could be taken; in fact, much was omitted in his various journeys which would, no doubt, be very interesting to a large class of travellers, and there is a good deal done in England which, to persons who have no rural taste, had better be omitted; and it might not be amiss to say here that the author's tour in England was mainly to see all the country places worth seeing, large or small, and in mentioning these he has been led to go into more detail in their description than is consistent with the original intention of these guides; and he has been induced to do this solely for the sake of calling the attention of those travellers interested in such matters to these very extraordinary places—such as Elvaston Castle, Biddulph Grange, Alton Towers, Levens Hall, etc.—

which, being off the common line of travel, and not usually mentioned in English guide-books, would not otherwise be known; secondly, to see all the cathedrals; thirdly, the university and school towns; and fourthly, the various watering-places and spas. In accomplishing these several objects, it was necessary to go over the length and breadth of England, across country, by post as well as by rail; and although, as before said, the English route might have been better, yet the author cannot but think that any one following his footsteps would see and know more of England than most Englishmen, and quite as much as any American traveller would care to know. The same is true, in a more limited extent, perhaps, of Spain and the northern countries. The old track through France, Italy, Germany, and Switzerland, is so well beaten that it has been omitted.

As to the expense of these journeys, it must, of course, depend very much upon the purse and inclination of the traveller. The prices mentioned in these tours were for a party of four, without reference to expense, having always the best apartments at hotels, with private meals invariably, and the best conveyances, either rail or carriage—not, however, including extras, wines, or amusements—and during the years 1866-'68. Of course, four persons might travel at much less cost, by taking cheaper conveyances—occasionally, second-class carriages on the railways, and their meals at a *table d'hôte*. It must, however, be understood that four persons can travel cheaper than two, or even one, in proportion, for various reasons not necessary to mention here.

In conclusion, the author would simply remark that these little tours—the one through England being especially horticultural, calling attention to certain country places seldom visited or even known to Americans—are particularly intended to assist those who have not time or interest enough to work out their own journey (a matter always sufficiently perplexing), and who are willing to be satisfied with seeing what the writer has seen. The time-tables of the various railways and boats have, of course, changed, and it would be necessary to alter the journey as far as this; but the time, of course, is always the same in making the journey, though the hours may have changed. The season of the year when these journeys were made has been retained in the guides, as the best for the different tours, though by no means necessary.

H. W. S.

WODENETHE, Fishkill-on-Hudson, 1870.

SKELETON TOURS.

FIRST TOUR.

ENGLAND, IRELAND, SCOTLAND, AND WALES.

(*For Four Persons.*)

	£	s.
Aug. 18.—Breakfast at Queenstown. Walk about the town. Take steamer at 9.30 up the River Lea to Cork, 13 miles, in preference to rail. Lunch at Imperial Hotel, after which drive in jaunting-car to Blarney Castle and to the Groves of Blarney, seeing yews 700 years old, and an *Araucaria* 15 feet high. Expenses at Queenstown, custom-house fees, and breakfast, ...	2	5
Aug. 19.—Walk or drive about the town, seeing the churches; drive to the country-place of Mr. Leigh. Beautiful *Araucarias, Pinus insignis, Thæpsis,* etc.; exquisite flower-garden.		
Aug. 20.—About town in the morning; after lunch, in a jaunting-car to Black Rock Castle,	2	5

and to Mr. Pike's place—very beautiful flowers. Back by Cemetery, seeing Father Matthew's grave—car, ...   £ s.
2 5
  10

Aug. 21.—Leave Cork for Youghal, by rail, at 9.40, reaching Youghal at 10.45. Drive through the town to Sir Walter Raleigh's house, where the first potatoes were planted, and the yew-trees, where Sir Walter smoked his pipe to the horror of his servants, who, thinking him on fire, poured water over him. The house very quaint, with walls and fireplaces panelled in black Irish bog-oak. See St. Mary's Church, founded in the eleventh century. At 2, taking boat, steam up the Blackwater, with exquisite views and places; arrive at Cappaquin at 4; where, taking a jaunting-car, drive through "Belmont," Sir John Kane's, a grand old place, with some fine cedars of Lebanon, to the monastery at Mallory, 4 miles, containing 100 Trappists, vowed to perpetual silence; thence, 4 miles farther, to Lismore, where dine and sleep at the Devonshire Arms. Fare to Youghal, 12s.; lunch and car, 12s.; boat, 6s.; car, 12s., ...   2 2

Aug. 23.—Visit Lismore Castle, a splendid restoration by the late Duke of Devonshire, and also to a most exquisite little place belonging to Mr. Baldwin; at 12, take cars to Fermoy, 12 miles, and back to Cork. Expenses at Lismore, ...   1 12

Aug. 24.—Leave Cork in posting-carriage, at 9.30, passing through the finest possible scenery.   6 9

About 1, reach Inchigeelagh to lunch (wonderfully situated, in the wildest and most extraordinary scenery). Soon after starting, at 2, pass the lake of Gongane-Barra, where whoever bathes in its waters is saved from all diseases, and enter the far-famed pass of Keeiman Eigh, perhaps one of the wildest and most savage in the world, about 2 miles long, and celebrated as the place where the O'Learys and O'Sullivans, after they were outlawed, lived for centuries, preying upon strangers and their neighbors, and where the illicit distilleries are even now concealed. It was in this pass, also, that the White Boys destroyed the royal troops by throwing rocks down upon them. Proceeding round the head of the beautiful Bay of Bantry, reach Roche's Hotel, at Glengariff, at 8 P. M., having posted 66 miles from Cork, changing horses only once. Bill at Cork, five days, £10 10s.; post-horses to Killarney, £6 15s., ... £ 6 s. 9 . . . . 17 5

Aug. 25.—At Glengariff. . . . .

Aug. 26.—Leave Glengariff at 9, in posting-carriage, passing Cromwell's Bridge and ascending the mountains for 4 miles, until, after passing through a tunnel 600 feet long, you come suddenly upon the kingdom of Kerry, the whole property for 20 miles belonging to the Marquis of Landsdown. Arrive at 12.30, through the most sublime views of the Killarney and Kerry Mountains, at Kenmare, where lunch at the Landsdown Arms. Visit the convent, where beautiful Irish lace may be 23 14

bought. Starting again at 3, reach the Victoria Hotel at Killarney at 8. Bill at Glengariff, £4 10s.; lunch at Kenmare, 10s., ... £ s.
23 14
5 0

Aug. 27.—Take a four-oared boat and bugler at 9; row to Ross Castle; built in twelfth century; destroyed in the civil war by Cromwell; once the stronghold of the O'Donahue, whose spirit still appears once in seven years. Thence, by Lady Kenmare Cottage, through the Wier Bridge to Eagle's Nest, where the bugle-echoes are most beautiful; to upper lake, where lunch, returning at 1 to Mucross, O'Sullivan's Cascade, and Innisfallen, perhaps the most beautiful spot in the world; an island of 21 acres, with magnificent park-trees; a thorn 140 feet in circumference (the head), and a holly 14 feet in circumference (the stem); a splendid old abbey in ruins, built in seventh century. Return at 5 P. M. . . . .

Aug. 28.—Walk through Lord Kennard's grounds, and, after lunch, by jaunting-car to Mucross Abbey, a most charming and well-preserved ruin, 800 years old. In the centre of the cloisters is a yew coeval with the abbey, 10 feet in circumference (the trunk), and said to be the highest in Europe. Afterward, home to dinner, through Mr. Herbert's grounds. For those who have time or inclination, a very agreeable excursion may be made through the Gap of Dunloe and Kate Kearney's Cottage. .

Aug. 29.—Leave Killarney at 10.30, by train. Reach Limerick, Cruise's Royal Hotel, at 2.30. 28 14

	£	s.

See the cathedral, built in 1100, partly destroyed by Cromwell; very ancient and interesting, especially the tombs of the O'Briens; also the old castle built by King John. Bill (two days) at Killarney and boat, ... 28 14

. . . . . 7 15

Aug. 30.—Leave Limerick at 12. Reach Dublin at 6, Gresham Hotel. Bill at Limerick, 2 10
Fare by rail to Dublin and car, . . . 3 10

Aug. 31.—Take car and drive round the town to Bank of Ireland, the different churches, the city hall, the Four Courts, the Custom-House, Trinity College, with fine portraits in the dining-hall of Queen Elizabeth and Dean Swift.

Sept. 1.—Take car at 9.30 and drive to Phœnix Park. See the viceregal lodge and the Chief Secretary's house, also the castle, where the chapel and state apartments are very fine. See Glas Nevin Cemetery.

Sept. 2.—Sunday, to St. Patrick's Cathedral, where Dean Swift once officiated. After lunch, to Bray by rail—a celebrated watering-place—here, taking a car, drive to Lord Monck's and Lord Powerscourt's; dine at Bray; back to Dublin by train at 8. Expenses to and from Bray, 16s.; dinner, £1 3s.; car, 10s., . . 2 9

Sept. 3.—Go by train at 10.30 to Maynooth. See the Institution, and also Carton near by, the residence of the Duke of Leinster, with most beautiful grounds and superb trees, especially cedars of Lebanon; the house charmingly situated, over an Italian garden, and in view

44 18

of a splendid park, the vases in the garden being enclosed in wicker-work. Back to Dublin at 5. Expenses, rail, ...   £ s.
44 18
12

To those disposed to go to the Giant's Causeway, *via* Belfast, and return to Dublin, the time occupied would be about four days. Bill at Dublin, one week, four persons, . . .   23 6

Sept. 4.—Leave Dublin at 6 A. M. and Kingstown at 7, by boat, reaching Holyhead at 11, and by train in an hour to the Menai Bridge. George Inn, one of the best in England, in full view of the suspension bridge. After lunch, take a carriage and drive to Bangor, a quaint old town, and to Penryn Castle, seeing the model cottages, the old church, and splendid yew avenue, 150 years old. Back to dinner. Fare from Dublin to Holyhead, ...   3 16

Sept. 5.—Leave the hotel at 9 in carriage, 8 miles to Carnarvon, a splendid old castle, built in 1283 by King Edward I., and in fine preservation. Then 9 miles farther, through the grand pass of Llanberris, one of the most remarkable in Europe, in full sight of Snowdon, 3,571 feet high, returning to the George Inn to dine. Expenses and lunch, . . .   1 15

Sept. 6.—By carriage to Plas Newyd, seat of the Marquis of Anglesea; a fine park, grand trees, and superb views of the Snowdon range; also to Beaumorris Castle, a very interesting ruin, built by Edward I., and having 26 towers. Return to the George to lunch. Taking train at 2.15, reach Chester at 5 (Queen's Hotel),   74 7

where see the cathedral, built (a large portion) in 875, also some of the old streets and houses.	£ s. 74 7
Bill at the George Inn, two days, . . .	9 17

Sept. 7.—Take a carriage and drive to Eaton Hall, the Marquis of Westminster, a short distance from Chester; the place very grand and stately. A very fine specimen of *Araucaria imbricata* here. Back to Chester to lunch, after which drive 2 miles or so, to Hoole House, Mrs. Hamilton's, formerly Lady Broughton's, famous for its rock-work for over 30 years; a little lawn, of less than an acre, surrounded by a rockery over 40 feet high; planted with clipped yews, *Araucarias*, etc.; 28 circular beds of raised baskets on the lawn. The whole kept in most exquisite order. Cab, 18s.; fees, 3s.,   1 1

Sept. 8.—Sunday; to the cathedral in the morning, and to St. John's Church in the afternoon—the oldest in Chester, founded in 689; after service, round the walls and through the old arcades. Bill at Chester, . . .   8 17

Sept. 9.—Leave Chester by rail for Liverpool at 9 (the Adelphi); fare, ...   12
where, taking carriage, drive 8 miles to Knowsley, Earl of Derby's, first getting a pass at your banker's, which will occupy two to three hours to see; the stables being especially fine, a quadrangle of 200 feet square, enclosing a paved yard; in the centre a place for washing carriages; beyond, a circle in straw for exercising horses, each pair of horses being kept in boxes, in a separate stable; 30 pairs, the best   94 14

costing 800 guineas; 35 grooms, 6 coachmen. The gardens contain 9 acres; require, with the ornamental grounds, 35 men and 5 women. The park is 12 miles in circumference, and the deer-park 14 miles, the latter containing 8,000 deer. There are 25 lodges and gates, and 50 other cottages and houses. On the drive back to Liverpool, see Botanic Garden. . . .   £ s.
   94 14

Sept. 10.—Walk or drive through the town, seeing the docks, Exchange, and the park at Birkenhead, ...

Sept. 11.—Leave Liverpool (bill), . .   7 10
at 9, by train, reaching Boness, on Lake Windermere, at 12.45. (The Queen's.) After lunch take steamer at 2.30 and make the entire circumference of the lake, 11 miles long. The portion about Ambleside and the Little River at the other end being particularly beautiful. Fare, Liverpool to Boness, ...   3 6

Sept. 12.—By carriage 12 miles to Levens Hall, near Milnthrop, an old Elizabethan mansion, a part built in the eleventh century; the furniture, hangings, etc., all belonging to this period; a fine old servants' hall in oak, with an immense fireplace, six to eight feet wide, and 1582 over it; with long tables and benches round the sides for the servants' meals. Above this, a baronial hall panelled in oak, heavily carved and hung in leather, with exquisitely-emblazoned windows, square bays, in small diamond and hexagon patterns, set in lead; an oak floor with a square of Turkey carpet   105 10 in the centre. Armor, boar-spears, and saddles, etc., about the room. This opened by three descending steps into the drawing-room, so beautifully carved in wood that, at present prices of labor, it is estimated the same work would cost £3,000. This also hung in gilded and embossed leather, and from which opened several quaint and curious rooms similarly treated and hung. In some were concealed doors, behind the arras leading by dim and mysterious corridors to obscure chambers. The gardens equally wonderful, seven acres being devoted to topiary work, most of it planted and first clipped by Beaumont, gardener to James I., and generally of yew and box, and some holly, from twelve to thirty feet high. There are also pleached alleys, as described by Shakespeare, divided by beech-hedges thirteen feet high, and the arches twenty. The grass walks or alleys laid down 250 years ago, on slate beds eight inches below the surface, and perfectly level, like a billiard-table, used for bowling-greens. Back to Boness to dinner,

£	s.
105	10

Sept. 13.—Leave Boness in posting-carriage at 9, passing up the lake by Ellery, where Wilson, and afterward Colonel Hamilton, author of "Cyril Thornton," lived, by Rydal Lake and Rydal Mount (Wordsworth's house), Grassmere, Raise Gap, Thorlmere Lake, Legerthrait to Keswick, 23 miles. After lunch, drive with another carriage round Derwentwater, by Barrow House and Barrow Falls, the Bowder

105 10

Stone, Lowdore Falls, Rorthrait, Setollers. About three hours' drive—if time, extend drive three hours longer to Honister Pass, Gates, Grath, Buttermere, Crumlock Lake, and Vale of Newland, back to Keswick to dine and sleep, . £ 105 s. 10

Sept. 14.—Walk to Greta Hall (Southey's residence), and leaving Keswick at 10. In carriage drive past the head of St. John's Vale, Threlkeld, Moor End, Mell Fell, Matterdale, with a splendid yew, Docray, Gow-Barrow park, very grand, with fine views of Ulswater, Lyulph's Tower, with a quaint old dining-room, in oak, Ara-force Fall, Patterdale, where dine at Brownrigg's, an excellent inn. At 4, starting again by Brother's Lake, over the Kirkstone Pass, where is the highest inhabited house in England, 1,470 feet above the lake. Reach Boness by Troutbeck, and Crook's house to tea. Bill at Keswick, and Patterdale, . . . 4 4

Nothing can well be finer than these lakes, mountains, and drives, except those at Killarney, which are grander, though not as soft and beautiful. In Patterdale churchyard is a yew perhaps a 1,000 years old, and 18 feet in circumference, ...

Sept. 15.—Leave Boness at 5¾ for Penrith; after waiting one and a half hours for a connection at Oxenham, reach Penrith (The Crown) at 9. Bill at Boness, £13 14; fare to Penrith, £1 15s., ... 15 9

Sept. 16.—Taking posting-carriage, drive to ——— Brougham Hall, Lord Brougham's, and also to 125 3

	£	s.

Lowther Castle, the latter very magnificent, with a fine collection of pictures, especially Hogarth's, and a splendid park of 600 acres. Leaving Penrith at 1.23 by rail, reach Edinburgh at 5.45. Windsor Hotel, in Moray Place. Expenses at Penrith and to Edinburgh, ...   125 3

 . . . . 4 10

Sept. 18.—Take a carriage-drive through Princes and George Streets, to the Castle, Grassmarket, Cannongate, St. Giles, Parliament House and Square, John Knox's House, and Holyrood Palace, seeing Queen Mary's apartment and the scene of Rizzio's murder. Back along the Queen's drive, by Salisbury Crags and Arthur's seat, Dean Bridge, Heriot's Hospital, the Cowgate, very extraordinary for the denseness of its population, carriage, . . .   15

Sept. 19.—Leave Edinburgh at 9.40, by North British Rail for Melrose, 37 miles, where, taking cab, drive three miles to Abbotsford, see house and gardens, a wall of yew, thirteen years planted, with medallions set in, being especially fine. Back to Melrose to lunch, afterward to the Abbey (close to the inn), founded in 1136; and by fly four miles to Dryburgh Abbey, founded in 1150, with a yew of the same age. Return to Edinburgh by rail at 5.30. Fare to Melrose and back, £2 10s; fees, 3s.; lunch, 4s., ...   2 17

Sept. 20.—Leave Edinburgh at 1.20 by train, reaching Stirling at 2.15; visit the castle with one of the finest views. Take another train at   132 5

5.25, go on to Callender at 6, to dine and sleep (The Dreadnought). Bill at Edinburgh, three days, £7 15s.; fare to Callender, £1 5s., . . £132 5s 9d 0

Sept. 21.—Leave Callender in posting-carriage at 9, reaching the inn at the Trossachs at 11. Walk over the mountain to the celebrated pass of Aberfoil, to Bailie Nicol Jarvie Inn, the Clachan of Aberfoil, and back to the Trossachs to dine and sleep. Bill at Callender, . . 2 15

Sept. 22.—Leave the Trossachs at 9.30, in carriage for Loch Katrine, taking steamer at 11; sail down the lake, passing Ellen's Isle and the "Silver Strand," reaching the upper end of the lake at 12.30; take a carriage, and drive five miles through a narrow pass to Inversnaid, where lunch, and on by boat at 2; down Loch Lomond, reaching Ballock at end of lake at 15 minutes to 4; hence by rail to Glasgow at 5.10. (George Hotel.) Bill at Trossachs, £3 4s. Fare on Loch Katrine, 10s. Lomond, 10s., ... 4 4

Sept. 23.—Sunday to the Cathedral, after which to the University, very gloomy; and to the park, ...

Sept. 24.—About the town, and at 1.30 by rail 9 miles to Hamilton Palace, the Duke of Hamilton's, grandson of Beckford, the author of "Vateck;" the Palace most stately and magnificent, the front being a specimen of an enriched Corinthian order, with a projecting pillared portico, after the style of the Temple of Jupiter Stator at Rome, 264 feet in length, 149 4 and 60 in height. In the mausoleum a constant fire day and night is kept up. The avenue here is particularly fine. Taking a carriage, drive to Barncluith, with clipped terrace gardens in the Dutch style, planted in 1679, on quaint stone battlements, also Cadzow Forest, with splendid oaks, 35 to 36 feet in circumference, and having some 60 to 80 of the Scottish wild-oxen yet left. Back to Glasgow, to dine and sleep. Bill at Glasgow, 4 days, £10 11s.; cab and rail, £1 4s., ... 12 15

	£	s.
	149	4

Sept. 25.—Leave Glasgow at 7 o'clock A. M., in steamer, reaching Greenock at 9, where the beauties of the Clyde begin to appear, passing Dumbarton and its castle, Dunoon, Rothesay, and through the Kyle of Bute, a charming strait through the islands, and filled with fishing-smacks, for the Loch Fine herrings, which are very celebrated. Arrive at Ardescraig at 2, where change to a boat on the Crinan Canal; after a beautiful sail of 9 miles, again change to another steamer, where, dining, pass through the Dorishtmore, or Great Gate between the chain of islands Jura, Isla, Scarba, and the Mull, Iona and Staffa at a distance, reach Oban, beautifully situated in a circular bay, at 7 P. M. Here, if wishing to visit Staffa, sleep; otherwise proceed in steamer, reaching Banavie at 10 P. M. Passage to Inverness, . 6 10

Sept. 26.—Rise early, to see the effect of the sun on Ben Nevis, 4,428 feet high, immediately in front of the inn; walk 2 miles to Inverlochy 168 9

Castle, scene of the battle between Argyll and Montrose in 1645. Breakfast at 7; leave in steamer on the canal at 8, until you reach Loch Lochy, 10 miles, passing the ancient castle of the Camerons, also the burial-place of the Lochiels, then through a second canal to Loch Oich, 3 miles long, passing Achnacarry, belonging to the Lochiel, and Invergarry Castle, as well as the monument erected by Colonel McDonald, of Glengarry, to the seven heads of his seven cousins, which he cut off for murdering the two sons of the chief of the clan—McDonald himself being the original of the Fergus McIvor, of Sir Walter Scott's "Waverley;" thence by another canal to Loch Ness, 24 miles long, scenery fine, though not so grand as yesterday's. To Foyer's, where an hour to see the falls, very picturesque, by Urquart Castle, a splendid ruin in a magnificent position, with an arrangement for pouring molten lead on its assailants, and a charming old Scotch residence, Aldowrie House, where Sir James McIntosh was born; reach Inverness (the Caledonian Hotel) at 5 P. M. Bill at Banavie, and lunch, ... £ 168 9 s. 1 12

See Macbeth's Castle, splendidly situated on an eminence overlooking the town and river.

Sept. 27.—Leave Inverness at 10.18, passing Culloden, where the battle was fought; Cawdor Castle, once belonging to the Thane of Cawdor of Macbeth, and now to the Earl of Cawdor, Longmuir, the supposed blasted heath, 170 1

	£	s.

where Macbeth and Banquo met the weird sisters, Birnam wood, etc., to Blair Castle, where leave the train. After lunch visit the grounds. The walks and drives of this estate are said to extend 50 miles; the larch-plantations cover 11,000 acres, and number of trees planted, 27,000,000. Glen Tilt, belonging to the duke, alone contains 100,000 acres, and 10,000 head of red deer, 5,000 acres being preserved for grouse, 20,000 for deer, and 30,000 for deer-stalking. There still remain 8 or 10 of the original larch from which all Scotland, England, Ireland, and America, were planted, one of the largest measuring $16\frac{1}{2}$ feet in circumference, with a head and branches as spreading as a cedar of Lebanon. Taking carriage at the inn, drive or walk through the celebrated pass of Killiecrankie to Ballinling, passing Grand Tully, an old Scotch castle, said to be the original of the Tully Veolan of "Waverley," and Glenquoich, the home of Fergus McIvor; and reaching Aberfeldie (Breadalbane Arms) to dine and sleep. Bill at Inverness, £2 1s.; to Aberfeldie, £4 10s., ...   170   1

6 11

Lunch and carriage at Blair, ...   1   5

Sept. 28.—Sunday at Aberfeldie.

Sept. 29.—Walk to the falls of Moness and Birks of Aberfeldie, a beautiful ravine and fall celebrated by Burns, and after lunch walk to Castle Menzies, a quaint old Scotch castle with pepper-pot towers on the angles and most extraordinary beeches and planes, forming com-   177 17 plete arbors; the collection of new evergreens very complete here, ... 177 17

Sept. 30.—In morning, drive or walk to Grand Tully Castle, the residence of Sir William Stewart, the actual original of Sir Walter Scott's Tully Veolan, with secret passages and communications through the walls. After lunch drive 5 miles to Taymouth Castle, the magnificent residence of the Marquis of Breadalbane, a splendid castle 800 feet front, in a park, consisting of a valley between two ranges of mountains, five miles long by three broad, with superb groups and masses of trees, one beech in particular measuring 43 feet in circumference four feet from the ground, said to be the largest in Scotland; the estate being 120 miles long by 3 to 15 broad. At the end of the park is Loch Taymouth, 16 miles long. Bill and expenses at Abergeldie, . . 5 12

Oct. 1.—Leave Abergeldie in train at 8.15, reaching Perth at 11, and Edinburgh via Sterling at 1. From Perth you may branch off to Aberdeen and Balmoral.

Oct. 2.—Leave Edinburgh (Royal Hotel), at 10 in fly, for Dalkeith Palace, seat of the Duke of Buccleuch; see palace, filled with splendid pictures of the family. The grounds are very fine, and the stables especially so, containing some 90 horses when the family is at home, 30 of which are valuable hunters, costing 200 to 300 guineas each. In the palace is the state bed, used in 1633 by Charles I., in 1822 by 183 9

George IV., and in 1842 by Queen Victoria. £ *s.*
From here drive to Roslyn Castle and Ros- 183 9
lyn Chapel, the first containing subterranean
passages in the rocks, where Bruce lived in
concealment. A beautiful walk conducts to
the chapel, built 595 years ago, and by far the
most exquisite in style and carvings in Scotland, perhaps in England. Back by 5 o'clock.
Cab, £1; fees, 5s.; lunch, 5s., . . . 1 10
  See Botanic Garden, with very fine collection of plants.

  Oct. 5.—Leave Edinburgh at 10.15 by North British Rail, passing near the sea and some splendid views, through and over Newcastle to Durham by 2.20; here stop. After lunch at the Three Tuns, visit the Cathedral, founded in 1072, 365 feet long and 92 feet high, a magnificent building; afterward to the Castle, a splendid old palace, black with age, said to have been built by William the Conqueror. Bill at Edinburgh, three and a half days, £9 2s.; fare to Durham, £5 10s., ... 14 12

  Oct. 6.—Leave Durham at 11, reaching Ripon at 2.20 (The Unicorn), where taking a carriage, drive to Studley Royal, Earl de Grey, and Ripon, containing in the park the magnificent ruins of Fountain Abbey. Here are some Norway spruce 130 feet high. The Abbey originally covered 12 acres, and much is well preserved, though founded 1,000 years ago. Here also are some yews 1,400 years old,

199 11

	£	s.

27 feet in circumference, which sheltered the monks when building the abbey. Bill at Durham, £1 10s.; fare to Ripon, £2 10s., . .   199 11

                                                              4   0

Oct. 7.—Walk to Cathedral, being restored, but a fine building, 320 feet long. Leave Ripon by train at 10.30, reach Harrogate at 11.30, and York at 1.30 (The York House). See the Cathedral, by many thought the finest in England, 500 odd feet long, by nearly 100 feet high, founded in the fourteenth and fifteenth centuries; the great east window, 80 feet high, was painted by a man who undertook to do it in three years, at six shillings a week. Bill at Ripon, £2 13s.; fare to York, £1 10s., ...   4   3

Oct. 8.—At York, seeing the Cathedral and old houses; at 2 drive to Hesslington Hall, an old Elizabethan mansion of red brick, with old clipped yew-trees, 200 years old. Bill at York, 4 days, £10 2s.; fare to Scarborough, £1 5s., ...   11 7

Oct. 9.—Leave York at 9.30 in train, sending luggage to Scarborough; stop at Castle Howard station, take 'bus to the Castle—Earl of Carlisle. The house very fine, built by Sir John Vanbrugh, and the park, with four splendid avenues meeting in the centre, planted by the third earl, 150 years ago. The pictures and statues, both within and without the house, are superb. On by a later train to Scarborough (The Crown), to dine and sleep. 219 1

Oct. 10.—Walk on the esplanade and about the town. £ *s.* 219 1

Oct. 11.—Sunday.

Oct. 12.—Bill at Scarborough, 6 days, . 21 6

Oct. 13.—Leave Scarborough at 2.30, reaching Leeds at 5.30 (Bull and Mouth, very bad); see the town (Station Hotel best), . . .

Oct. 14.—By train at 9.30, 17 miles to Keighley, then 4 miles by carriage to Haworth, a straggling village with one long street, to the Parsonage House, where lived the Brontés, Charlotte, Anne, and Maria, authoresses of "Jane Eyre," "Villette," "Wuthering Heights," etc.; here old Mr. Bronté, the incumbent of Haworth, lived 41 years on £150 a year, and died at 85, having outlived all his children. Expenses, ... 1 5
Back to Leeds to dine and sleep.

Oct. 15.—Leave Leeds at 10.30 in train, reaching Rotherham at 11.30; taking a fly, drive 4 miles to Wentworth House, Earl Fitzwilliam, the most magnificent house, perhaps, in England, 906 feet front; the state apartments very grand, the dining-room very superb, being 50 feet square, the ground hall 50 by 75, and 30 feet high; all the three drawing-rooms very ornate and superbly gilded, with charming pictures. See the chamber and dressing-room of Lord Strafford, who was beheaded. The stables even finer than Knowsley (Earl of Derby's); the gardens are very stately. From ———
Rotherham to Sheffield, 5 miles in fly, then by 241 12

train, half an hour to Worksop (The Lion). Bill at Leeds, £3 12s.; fly to Wentworth, 14s., ...

£ s.
241 12
4 6

Oct. 16.—Drive in carriage 4 miles, to Clumber Park, seat of the Duke of Newcastle, beautifully situated with its Italian gardens, extending over a lake filled with wild-fowl. A mile or so farther to Thoresby, Earl Manvers, with a fine effect of avenue, passing through a part of the park or chase called Bithagne and Birkland, being the oldest portions of Sherwood Forest; huge oaks, 1,000 years old, averaging 30 to 40 feet in circumference, with a thick undergrowth of fern, through and amidst which are numerous deer; nothing in England is perhaps grander or wilder than this forest of nearly 15,000 acres, with innumerable sylvan glades. Passing through Clipstone Park, where King John had a palace, lunch at the little inn famous for its home-brewed. Returning from here, drive through a part of Welbeck Park, Duke of Portland, seeing the abbey at a distance, and the ornamental water, unfinished in 1868, of over 200 acres. The park contains 2,083 acres, and some remarkable oaks, of which the most celebrated are the Two Porters, one being 100 feet high and 40 in circumference, the other 90 by 36; the Seven Sisters, 88 feet high, circumference 80 feet. The Greendale oak in 1724 had an opening large enough to allow a carriage or three horsemen abreast to pass through, the circumference above the

245 18

arch, 35 feet 3 inches, height of the arch, 10 feet, width 6 feet 3 inches, supposed to be 1,000 years old. Some oaks which have been cut down were found to be 1,200 years old. From Welbeck to Worksop Manor, Lord Foley's, and back to Worksop to dine and sleep. Bill at Worksop, £5 15s.; fare to Lincoln, £1 4s.; to Boston, £1 4s.; cab, 10s.,

Oct. 17.—Leave Worksop by train at 9.20, reaching Lincoln at 11; take cab and drive to the Cathedral, finer even than York, tower 266 feet high, length only six inches less than York. Leave Lincoln at 3.30, reaching Boston (The Peacock), at 5,

Oct. 19.—Ascend the tower of St. Botolph's, with a magnificent view of Lincolnshire. Leave Boston by train at 10, reach Grantham at 11.30; taking a fly, drive 8 miles to Belvoir Castle, the Duke of Rutland's superb estate, with magnificent rooms and pictures; from here at 4, by train to Nottingham, 17 miles, George IV. inn. Bill at Boston, £4 10s.; fare to Grantham, £1 1s.; fly to Belvoir Castle and back, £1 10s.; to Nottingham, 10s.,

Oct. 20.—Leave Nottingham at 10, in carriage with post-horses, 11 miles to Newstead Abbey (Lord Byron's), passing Westwell Hall, Duke of St. Alban's. Newstead, very interesting, on a lake, the older parts of the abbey beautifully preserved, and the Italian gardens exquisite. The monument (tomb) to the memory of the poet's dog Boatswain being very

£	s.
245	18
8	13
7	11
262	2

conspicuous; from Newstead 3 miles farther to Annesley Hall, where Mary Chaworth, Byron's first love lived; a beautiful park of 800 acres, an old Elizabethan house, with heavy mullioned windows and court-yards; a most charming Italian garden, heavy stone balustrades and pilasters, with large stone balls on top; an old church immediately adjoining and in connection with the house, 900 years old. Mary Chaworth's flower-garden exists just as it did in her day, and a little oaken door in the garden wall still shows the marks of Lord Byron's balls, who used it as a target. From here 2 miles to Hucknel, where, in the old church, built in 1100, is a mural tablet, with the simple inscription, " George Gordon, Lord Byron of Rochdale, Author of Childe Harold's pilgrimage, born in London, 1786, died at Missolonghi, 1824." From here to Wollaton Hall, Lord Middleton's, a superb, ornate, though gloomy house, with a splendid avenue and numerous deer. Back to Nottingham by 5, where, taking the train, reach Derby (The Royal) at 6. Bill at Nottingham, £2 7s.; carriage to Newstead, £1 15s.; lunch, 6s.; fare to Derby, 10s., . .

£   *s.*

262   2

4 18

Oct. 21.—Leave Derby by train at 10.30, for Borrowwash, 5 miles; walk or drive one mile to Elvaston Castle, Earl of Harrington, the most wonderful place in England, and probably in the world, for its topiary work, as well as collection of evergreens. Here are picea pinsapos 30 feet high, abies menzesii and douglasi

267 00

35 feet, hemlocks much finer than those in America. The grand entrance through the golden gates, opened only on state occasions, is bordered on one side by a variegated holly-hedge, with occasional standards of Irish yew, and on the other side (being divided by great masses of golden yew in a setting of common yew) is a line of golden and Irish yews, backed by a row of pinus nobilis; at end of each grass avenue is a superb golden yew, 20 feet high and as broad; from this you pass into three distinct and separate gardens, each more extraordinary than the other in size, and the figures of the topiary work. Entire cottages cut out of yew, yew-arbors 20 feet high, having a base 30 feet square, with a succession of steps; the top surmounted by two peacocks, 6 feet long and 3 or more feet high, the head and figures closely cut, while the tails, in golden yew, are allowed to remain unclipped and feathery. One very extraordinary house in yew, with several gables, is surmounted by two birds, one in a nest, the other attempting to fly out, each larger than the largest eagle. There are also perfectly green cones of English yew, 40 feet high, with golden heads (caps of golden yew), these standing in a double base or platform of English yew, 25 to 30 feet square, and 12 to 15 inches high, perfectly smooth and flat, as if made of slate; there are also long alleys of smooth turf bordered by alternate Irish and golden yews, the latter tied

close in by wires to keep them pyramidal, and surmounted by golden crowns; other avenues of Irish junipers and golden cypress. In one of the gardens (each divided from the other by clipped yew-hedges 20 feet high, with occasional arches) are groups of Chinese barrels, cut out of juniper; in this garden a fine effect is produced by a large circle, 100 feet in diameter, made of large triangles of alternating golden and green yews, dovetailing into each other, and kept down (6 inches high) so as to produce a brilliant parterre. One of the most effective things, however, is the Vandyk Walk, a covered, irregular walk through an arbor, thickened at the bottom by box, and close over the head, the light being admitted by occasional loop-holes. The ornamental water is also most charmingly managed; a lake of apparently endless extent, with the margin beautifully broken by occasional borders of smooth lawn, backed by artificial rock-work, and planted with golden and English yews, deodars, and araucarias; then again points of rough, ragged rock to the water's edge, in one case closely resembling a ruined castle, covered with moss and ivy, and the effect increased by broken mullioned window-bars set against one of the openings. At one end of the lake, after passing through a dense yew-walk, you come suddenly upon a large, round hole, 8 feet in diameter, in the rockery; through this you see the whole extent of the lake, with all its different

£	s.
267	00
267	00

points and islands, the softer parts in lawn with an occasional weeping birch or willow; the rougher with here and there a cedar of Lebanon or araucaria amidst the crags. Another beautiful effect is produced by a sudden vista through a cavern across the lake, to another vista through a cave, in which stands a mossy stone cross wreathed in silver ivy, duplicated in the lake by its reflection; and beyond this the vista is continued three miles through a dark fir-wood, until it terminates in Spondon Church spire. Back to Derby to dine and sleep, seeing also the Arboretum. Bill at Derby, £9 17s.; to Matlock, £1 10s., ...

	£	s.
	267	00
	11	7

Oct. 23.—Leave Derby by train at 9, reaching Matlock Bath at 9.40 (Temple Inn). Walk through the Cumberland Cavern, the largest in Derbyshire; after lunch, drive to Willersley Hall, the house of the original Arkwright; see the mill where the spinning-jenny was invented and first used; thence to Lea Hurst, the residence of Florence Nightingale, a pretty stone cottage in an estate of 5,000 acres. On still farther to Wingfield Manor, a grand old ruin of the time of Henry IV. Here Mary Queen of Scots was a prisoner nine years. Back to Matlock to dinner.

Oct. 23 and 24.—At Matlock.

Oct. 25.—Leave the hotel at 9.30 in carriage, reaching Hadden Hall, the Duke of Rutland's, 8 miles, at 11, one of the most interesting old places in England, built in the eleventh century, 278 7 and the original of Mrs. Radcliffe's "Mysteries of Udolpho." From here by Bakewell, famous for its sheep; to Chatsworth, 2 miles, lunching at the Edensor Inn at the gate, after which see the house, gardens, great conservatory, etc., occupying about two hours, the wood-carvings in the house, by Gibbons, being very celebrated. Thirty men are kept in the ornamental grounds and 25 in the kitchen garden. Back to Matlock to dine. Lunch, 13s.; fees and tolls, 8s., ...

Oct. 26.—Leave Matlock by train at 9.45, reaching Buxton at 10.15; taking carriage, drive 14 miles through the bleakest and highest moors to Macclesfield to lunch, leaving Macclesfield at 3.30 in train, reach Congleton (Lion and Swan, very quaint) at 4; see the town. Bill at Matlock, and carriage to Chatsworth, ...

Fare to Buxton, 17s.; carriage to Macclesfield and lunch, ...

The Buxton moors, belonging to the Duke of Devonshire, are rented for shooting, at £12 the fortnight for each gun. Twelve gentlemen hire these moors for two weeks at this rate, and generally average 10 to 12 brace of grouse a gun each day. Each gun, therefore, pays a guinea a day, and shoots, or is supposed to, 10 pair of grouse.

Oct. 27.—Leave Congleton by train at 10, reaching North Rode at 10.20, waiting three-quarters of an hour and taking another train,

	£	s.
	278	7
	1	1
	8	8
	2	16
	290	12

reach Alton Towers, Earl of Shrewsbury's, at 11¾, the most ornate and Italian-looking place in England, a succession of beautiful terraces, with vases, statues, fountains, and flowers, superb trees both in variety and growth; the cedars of Lebanon on the slopes down to the lake are especially fine. Fare to and fro,

Oct. 28.—Leave Congleton in a carriage at 9.30, for Biddulph Grange, Mr. Bateman's, 4 miles, the most extraordinary place in England of its size; a Wellingtonia avenue, a beautiful pinetum, a rock; a Dutch, an Italian, and a stump garden—each concealed from the other; a wonderful Chinese garden, which you enter through a cave over a Chinese bridge, the garden being planted with Chinese plants and trees, and adorned with pagodas, monsters, idols, and other features of that country. There are 23 acres only of ornamental ground, and 15 men allowed to keep them up. Back to Congleton to lunch, after which, leaving Congleton at 4.30, reach Stoke-on-Trent at 4.50. Bill at Congleton, £3 11s.; fare to Stoke, 8s.,

Oct. 29.—Drive 3 miles from Stoke to Trentham, Duke of Sutherland's, by many esteemed the finest place in England, a beautiful park with majestic trees and fine hanging woods; the most exquisite pleasure-grounds, with grand masses of rhododendrons, azalias, mahonias, gaultherias, etc., with large, open glades of grass, down to a beautiful lake, one mile long; a succession of majestic terrace-gardens, with

£ s.
290 12

1 15

3 19

296 6

Italian balustrades to the water's edge; nothing
can be finer than the training of the pear-trees, 296 6
being in cup-form, as well as over umbrella
trellises; the grape and peach houses, only
4 feet wide by 12 high, the front glass being
as high as the back wall, thus having two sets
of plants. Back to Stoke to lunch; fly, 10s.;
bill at Stoke and fare to Stafford, £3 10s.   4 0
Leaving Stoke at 3, reach Stafford (The Vine),
to dine and sleep.

Oct. 31.—Taking a carriage, drive to Tixall
Hall, Sir T. Clifford's; Shugborough, Earl of
Lichfield's; Ingestrie, Earl of Shrewsbury's, and
Sandon, Earl of Harrowby's, 16 miles, fare, .   14

Of these places, Ingestrie was the finest
house about the period of the Tudors, with a
quantity of windows in bays and bows; the
park is very fine, being in large, umbrageous
masses, a superb beech avenue, 200 years old
and a mile long, some fine cedars of Lebanon
and Douglas firs, in the ornamental grounds.
The next best place being Sandon, where the
park is very undulating, and beautifully
clothed in splendid trees, especially beech.
Back to Stafford to dinner. Fly, . . .   14

Nov. 1.—Leave Stafford by rail at 11.15,
reaching Rugby at 11.45. Lunch at the Talbot
Arms, where the celebrated poisoning of Cook
and others took place by Palmer, in 1855,
Palmer's house being immediately opposite.
After lunch, drive in fly to Blithfield, Lord
Bagot's splendid old park and house, said—a 301 14

STAFFORD.] ENGLAND. [THE VINE.

portion of it—to have been built in the time of William the Conqueror. From here, 4 miles to Bishton, Lady Olivia Sparrow's, Woolsey Hall, Sir Charles Woolsey's, which has been in the same family 700 years, containing a fine oaken drawing-room and carved staircase; from here to Hagley Hall, Lady de la Zouch's, a picturesque old house. Fare to and from Stafford and fly, £1 1s.; lunch at Rugby, 15s. Back to Stafford to dine, ...

Nov. 2.—Leave Stafford at 11.15, reaching Lichfield at 12, remaining two hours for the cathedral, one of the most ornate in England, the pulpit and screen being of elaborately ornamented and twisted brass, with precious stones; the altar, most exquisite in alabaster, inlaid with precious stones; the monuments—Chantrey's cherubs and Hodson's tomb—very superb. Leaving Lichfield by train at 3, reach Rugby (George IV.) at 4, seeing the school and play-ground, famous in "Tom Brown," close by the hotel. Lunch at Lichfield, 9s.; fare to Lichfield 10s.; Lichfield to Rugby, £1 12s.,

Nov. 3.—Rugby school until 12, when by rail to Leamington (The Clarendon), in one hour; lunch and see the town. Bill at Rugby, £1 12s.; Rugby to Leamington, 12s.,

Nov. 4.—Leave Leamington by rail for Warwick, 2 miles; see Warwick Castle after lunch at the inn, drive in fly to Guy's Cliff, with a beautiful avenue of Scotch firs, 400 years old, best seen from the public road; also, some

	£	s.
	301	14
	1	16
	2	11
	2	4
	308	5

curious caves or recesses in the rocks; then 4   £   s.
miles farther to Kenilworth Castle. Back to 308   5
Leamington by fly to dine. Lunch and carriage, ...   1   0

Nov. 5.—Leave Leamington in carriage at 10, for Stratford, stopping at Warwick to see the Leicester Hospital, founded by Robert Dudley, Earl of Leicester, for a master and 12 old soldiers, they having each a parlor and bedroom, and £80 a year; the building and furniture are completely of the period of this foundation, 1573. See the identical chair for visitors used by James I. when he was entertained here. Drive 8 miles farther to Stratford-on-Avon, seeing Shakespeare's house and the church where he was buried. Back to Leamington by Charlecote, still owned by the Lucy family, where Shakespeare was tried for stealing deer; a fine old hall and grand park. Expenses, carriage and lunch,   . . .   2   0

Nov. 6–10.—At Leamington; excurse to Coventry and back, and to Stoneleigh Abbey, Lord Leigh's, a fine combination of an ancient and stately modern house, a beautiful Italian garden, sloping to the river with steps to the water; the park remarkable for its venerable trees, nearly as fine as Sherwood Forest; near the greenhouse a very fine *Taxodium sempervirens*, also fine *araucarias* and *Cryptomeria Japonica*, 30 feet high, ...

Nov. 11.—Leave Leamington by train at 10, ——
reaching Worcester, with three changes, at 1.50 311   5

(Star and Garter Inn); after lunch see cathe-dral, splendidly restored; here are the tombs of King John and Prince Arthur. Hard by the town the battle of Worcester was fought. Bill at Leamington, 6 days, £15; fare to Worcester, . | £ s.
311 5

16 15

Nov. 12.—Leave Worcester at 11.25 in train, reaching Malvern at 11.50. Taking fly, drive through the town to Malvern Wych, seeing a beautiful view, through a cutting in the rocks, of the two counties—Herefordshire on one side and Worcestershire on the other—from a height of 1,500 feet. From here to Madresfield Court, Earl of Beauchamp's, an interesting old place; the house with three gables, covered with ivy, surrounded by a moat filled with water; the intervening lawn beautifully planted with choice evergreens. Taking train at 3, reach Hereford (The Green Dragon), to dine and sleep. Bill at Worcester, £2 16s.; fare to Hereford, £1 8s., ... 4 4

See cathedral, with fine screen.

Nov. 13.—Leave Hereford at 9.40, passing Holm Lacey—a fine old Elizabethan mansion, where Pope wrote his "Man of Ross"—to Ross; where, taking a fly, drive to the church, where the "Man of Ross" is buried; then to the ruins of Goodrich Castle, built in 600—before the conquest. Afterward to Goodrich Court, Sir J. P. Merrick's, best imitation of an ancient castle in England, with furniture to correspond, and a splendid collection of armor. From here at 3, by train, to Cheltenham (the 332 4

Plough), *via* Gloucester, at 4. The view from the inn at Ross very fine. Bill at Hereford, £1 10s.; fare to Cheltenham, 15s.; fly to Goodrich and back, £1 2s., ... £ 332 *s.* 4

3 7.

Nov. 14.—Leave Cheltenham by train at 11 for Gloucester, where, taking a fly, drive to Highnam Court, Mr. Gambier Parry's, celebrated for its pinetum, perhaps the most complete in England, not excepting Dropmore. See Mr. Parry's church, built and adorned at his own expense, at a cost of £30,000, much of the painting and emblazoning being his own work. Back to Worcester, to the cathedral, built in 1047, containing the monuments of Edward II. and Robert of Normandy, son of the Conqueror; the east window, 87 feet high; the vault of the choir and the cloisters are considered the most beautiful in England. Return to Cheltenham at 4.40. Expense, . . . 1 2

Nov. 15.—At 12, drive 2 miles, to Southam House, Earl of Ellenborough's, a charming, quaint old Elizabethan house, built in 1628. On the summer-house is a glass star instead of a vane, which, in the sun, produces a very pretty effect. Rest of the day, see the town.

Nov. 16.—Leave Cheltenham at 11, reaching Bristol at 12.15, and, after half an hour's delay, Bath at 1.30 (York House). See the town, the park gardens, crescent, etc. Bill at Cheltenham, £12 16s.; fare to Bath, £2 3s., . . 14 19

Nov. 12.—Bath. Abbey Church, pump-room, etc.

351 12

	£	s.

Nov. 13.—Leave Bath at 10, in carriage, for Badminton, Duke of Beaufort's, 16 miles; a splendid house and park, with avenue 3 miles long, from Worcester Lodge. The duke, who is the present Nimrod of England, hunts every day, rain or shine, through the season, keeping 40 horses for this purpose. Back to Bath, by Codrington Hall, a fine old place. In the church at Badminton Lord Raglan, the English Commander-in-Chief in the Crimea, is buried. Here, also, is the monument to the Marchioness of Worcester, with its famous inscription, considered the most complimentary ever composed: 351 12

"Underneath this stone doth lie
As much virtue as could die;
Which, when alive, did vigor give
To as much beauty as could live."

Carriage to Badminton and expenses, . .   2 17

Nov. 14.—Leave Bath at 10.30, by train, for Chippingham; then, by fly, 5 miles to Bowood, Marquis of Lansdowne's, a beautiful Italian palace and superb place, especially rich in terraced gardens; a lake of 30 acres, with a fine pinetum, containing a Douglas fir 70-odd feet high. Five miles beyond Bowood is Lacock Abbey, a wonderful old place, said to be the best-preserved abbey "in residence" in England, founded in 1229, the cloisters, kitchen, and nuns' kitchen being very complete. Driving 3 miles farther, you come to Corsham House, Lord   354 9

Methuen's, a splendid house, with extraordinary yew-hedges, 30 feet thick and as high; the park planted by the celebrated Brown and the lake made by Repton. Back to Chippingham, then by rail to Bath to dinner. Expenses,

£ 354 / s. 9

. 1 7

Near Bath is Prior Park, where Fielding wrote "Tom Jones."

Nov. 15.—Leave Bath in train at 1.25, reaching Exeter (Royal) at 2.25. Walk about the town, seeing the old houses and the cathedral. Bill at Bath, £15; Bath to Exeter, £4 4s., . 19 4

Nov. 16.—Take a fly at 10, drive one mile to the celebrated nursery of Veitch & Co., seeing the famous pinetum-walk, with Douglas firs, cedars of Lebanon, *Cryptomerias*, *Taxodium*, etc., 30 feet high; also splendid cypress, *Goviana*, and *Macrocarpa*. Thence a mile in another direction, to the nursery and pinetum of Lucomb, Pince & Co., seeing, near the entrance, the celebrated Lucomb (evergreen) oak, the largest and finest in England, also the far-famed conifer rock-walk, of a quarter of a mile, between high, overhanging, artificial rocks, filled with every conceivable and known variety of evergreens, rock-plants, ferns, pampas-grass, *Arundos*, etc. Here is the first *Wellingtonia* planted in England, also the first *Thuja gigantea*, the one 25 × 30 feet, and the other about 12 feet high. This collection of evergreens is, perhaps, the finest in England. Near Exeter is Bicton, the celebrated place of Lady Rolle. Leaving

375 0

Exeter by train at 2.30, reach Torquay (the Royal) at 3.10. Bill at Exeter, £2 10s.; fare to Torquay, £1 6s., ...   £ s.
375 0
  3 16

Nov. 17.—Torquay for three weeks; one parlor and three fine chambers, with board for four persons in private apartment, £16 5s. a week—1866–'67.

Nov. 18.—At 10, taking a fly, drive to Babbicomb, Anstey's Cove, Bishopthorp, Watcomb, the seat of the late Mr. Brunell; the grounds beautifully laid out on a hill-side, and the valley exquisitely arranged with the most ornamental and rare trees and shrubs, even the cedar of Goa and *Yucca aloefolia* standing out all winter.

Nov. 19.—After lunch, drive to Berry Pomeroy Castle, a fine old ruin, charmingly draped in ivy.

Nov. 20.—Leave Torquay in train at 10.15 for Dawlish, 12 miles; then, by fly, 2 miles to Luscomb, beautiful house and grounds; then 4 miles to Mamhead. To an American, Mamhead is one of the most instructive places in England, as being sufficiently small and compact enough to be within the reach of an American ownership. The ornamental grounds, only seven acres, were kept in exquisite order (in 1866) by two men. Here are the finest *Abies morinda*, probably, in the country, 60 feet high, and very pendulous; also a mass of rhododendrons, 25 feet high and 150 feet in circumference, the earliest already in bloom, 378 16 in November. Although the park is only 70 acres, yet the groups and masses are so beautifully and artistically disposed, and the ground so undulating, and with such distant views of the sea and the river Exe, that it looks as if it might contain a thousand acres. The old church, with its magnificent old yew-tree, is quite the finest in rural beauty in the south of England. Back to Torquay to dine. Expenses,

Bill at Torquay, three weeks, and sundries, .

Dec. 13.—Leave Torquay by train at 11, reaching Exeter at 12.30 and Salisbury at 4.15 (White Hart). Walk to the cathedral. Torquay to Salisbury, ...

Dec. 14.—After seeing cathedral and bishop's palace, with pretty gardens, take carriage at 11 for old Sarum and Stonehenge, 9 miles across Salisbury Plain. Back by Wilton House, Earl of Pembroke's. See the splendid Vandyck-room, with perhaps the finest and largest sized pictures of this master to be found anywhere in one collection, most of them likenesses of the Pembroke family. In the gardens are the cedars of Lebanon planted by Sir Philip Sidney, it being at Wilton House he wrote his "Acadia." Near by is the church built by Lord Herbert of Lea, at a cost of £80,000. Back to Salisbury to dine. Expenses, . .

Dec. 15.—Leave Salisbury in train at 10 for Tisbury, 17 miles, where, taking a fly, drive to Wardour Castle, Earl of Arundel's, a fine house, with a very grand hall. Walk across the park

£	s.
378	16
2	7
53	15
5	16
1	15
442	9

to old Wardour Castle, a splendid ruin, magnificently clothed in ivy, and with the most superb cedars in England, except those at Warwick. Here Lady Blanche Arundel defended the castle for a fortnight, with a handful of men, against one thousand Parliament troops. From here, drive across the country to Fonthill, at present belonging to the Marquis of Westminster, once the celebrated residence of the eccentric Beckford, the talented author of "Vathek," the most gorgeous of Eastern stories. There are, however, no remains of the original Fonthill Abbey of Mr. Beckford's time, except a portion of the great tower; and to one not interested in Mr. Beckford's history and the extraordinary circumstances connected with the building of the abbey, this visit might be omitted. Back to Salisbury by 6. Expenses: fare to Tisbury, 18s.; carriage, 18s., . . 1 16

Dec. 16.—See cathedral again, the chapter-house being particularly fine. Leave Salisbury at 2.15, reaching Winchester (The George) at 3.33. Bill at Salisbury, three days, £9 2s.; Salisbury to Winchester, £1 4s., . . . 10 6

Dec. 17.—Winchester. See cathedral and Winchester school, etc.

Dec. 18.—Leave Winchester at 10.12 by train, reaching Basingstroke at 11, where, taking a fly, drive 6 miles to Strathfieldsaye, the Duke of Wellington's, a flat place, with a pretty river running through the lawn; a very plain yellow-stone house of two stories, simply fur-

£ s.
442 9

454 11

nished, with the same patterned carpet over the whole house, most of the chambers and some of the parlors being papered with engravings pasted on the walls. There is an avenue of yews here very good, and an interesting enclosure, where Copenhagen, the horse which the duke rode at the battle of Waterloo, is buried; the place generally of little pretension. Back to Winchester at 3. Expenses,

Dec. 19.—Bill at Winchester, four days, Leave Winchester by express train at 10.12, reaching London (Maurigy Hotel, Regent Street) at 12.9. Winchester to London,

	£	s.
	454	11
	2	0
	3	10
	2	6
	462	7

This trip, of about four months, of which three weeks were passed at Torquay and some two weeks at other places, might be accomplished in two months and a half; and in summer, with longer days, in proportionally shorter time. The expenses put down are simply those of hotels, carriages, and railroads. The author's actual expenses for extras, sundries, amusements, etc., were, for the period, £712.

SECOND TOUR.

ENGLAND.

(*For Three Persons.—Five Weeks.*)

April 8.—Leave London at 12, reaching Rochester (The Bull) at 1.15. After lunch take a cab; drive to Cobham House, Earl of Darnley's—splendid woods and park. Back by Gad's-hill House, residence of Charles Dickens. Scene of the celebrated robbery of Falstaff, in *Henry IV.*, by Prince Hal. Fare, . . . £ s.
15

April 9.—Visit cathedral. Around the town. Seeing Eastgate House—very quaint and ornate; also the old castle said to have been built by Julius Cæsar. At 12 take train for Canterbury, arriving at 1 (The Fountain). After lunch, take train for Margate, and then by fly, 4 miles, to Ramsgate; the former much the finest as a marine residence. Back to Canterbury at 7, to dine. Bill at Rochester, £1 14s.; fare and cab, £1 10s., ... 3 4

April 10.—Visit the cathedral; truly magnificent, especially the exterior, which is 4 feet 3 19 longer than York Minster, though not as wide. Seeing inside the nave, the spot where Thomas-à-Becket was slain in reign of Henry II., in 1160; also the tomb and monument, in brass, of Edward the Black Prince; with the original shield, coat-of-mail, and helmet with leopard crest, worn by the prince at the battle of Cressy, in 1350. After that, to St. Martin's, the first Christian church, founded in 187 by some Christians of the Roman army. Queen Bertha, the first Christian queen, was baptized here, in the same font they now use; and St. Augustin preached here. Erasmus, in visiting this cathedral in 1510, said: "Gold was the meanest thing to be seen. All shone and glittered with precious stones of extraordinary magnitude, some larger than the egg of a goose." After lunch, at 1, leave Canterbury, one of the quaintest of old towns, by train; reaching Tunbridge Wells, to tea. A lovely spot, and a charming hotel in a park (The Caverley). Bill at Canterbury, £2 2s.; to Tunbridge, £1 10s., .

£ s.
3 19

3 12

Both the Bull, at Rochester, and the Fountain, at Canterbury, are very comfortable, old-fashioned inns.

April 11.—Take train at 12 to Tunbridge, 5 miles; then drive by fly, 8 miles, to Knolle, the ancient seat of the Dukes of Dorset; now occupied by Countess Amherst. A grand old place, celebrated even in the time of the Conqueror—quite as old as Haddon; and the state apartments in perfect preservation. The fire-dogs

7 11

very handsome—those in King James's bedroom of solid silver; the bed-cover of cloth-of-gold, in scarlet tissue, cost £8,000; the mirrors, dressing-table, sconces, etc., like the fire-dogs, being of solid silver; the walls in tapestry costing £20,000. The pictures very interesting—many Knellers, Lelys, and the original of Sir Joshua Reynolds's "Gypsy Girl." Knolle has belonged to, and been inhabited at various periods by, Archbishop Cranmer, the Earl of Leicester, the Earl of Warwick, and many others. It is one of the oldest inhabited houses in England which retains its ancient furniture. The park is truly magnificent, 8 miles in circumference, with majestic trees; the Duchess's walk being very fine. Back to Tunbridge, to dine. Expenses, ... 1 5

April 12.—At Tunbridge. Seeing the town. Nothing can well be prettier than the situation of the Caverley Inn, or better kept—in a charming lawn, like a private place.

April 13.—At 10, taking a carriage, drive 5 miles, to Penshurst, the ancient seat of the Sydney family, and where Sir Philip Sydney was born, in 1554. In the park is the oak planted at his birth, to which Ben Jonson alludes as

" That tall tree, too, which of a nut was set
　At his great birth, where all the Muses met."

Penshurst, like Knolle, was of importance before the Conquest; and, after being in possession of several noble families, was presented by Edward IV. to Sir William Sydney in 1549,　8 16

£ s.
7 11

after the battle of Flodden Field. The young
Duke of Gloucester and his sister the Princess
Elizabeth, the children of Charles I., remained
a year here, under charge of the Countess of
Leicester, who was the mother of the "Sacharissa" of the poet Waller, and a beautiful avenue
in the park is named from her "the Sacharissa
Walk." Penshurst was also the birthplace of
Algernon Sydney, beheaded in the Tower in
1683. The mansion, like that of Knolle, encloses two courts. The fine old baronial hall
is 54 feet wide, by 38 long, and 62 high; having
a raised dais at the end, and three antique tables
for the servitors below. The fire was in the
centre of the hall, on an immense set of double
bars on high dogs of iron, rudely carved; the
smoke ascending through some flumes in the
ceiling. The most interesting apartments at
Penshurst are the rooms occupied by Queen
Elizabeth, where the furniture, bed, dressing-table, and toilet arrangements, remain precisely
as during the queen's visit—even to her ink-stand and card-table, embroidered by her own
hand. In the gallery is a bridle once used by
the Earl of Leicester. The park was once 6
miles in extent, but is now much reduced.
From Penshurst drive by same carriage 1½
miles to Redleaf, seat of William Wells, and
so celebrated by Loudon, in his magazine,
30 to 40 years ago. The place is still admirably kept up, and looks precisely as it does
in Mr. Loudon's illustrations. The flower-

£	s.
8	16
8	16

garden in diamond beds, edged with tile, is
the same — even the rustic houses are unchanged. The ornamental grounds are in as
exquisite order and as beautiful as it is possible
to conceive; about twelve acres, kept by nine
men, two of whom have worked here for fifty
years. At end of the lawn, separated by a wire
fence, is a beautiful rolling park of many hundred acres; and immediately near the rockery
is a charming lake. The collection of trees,
though not as large as many others, are much
more interesting from their size; being the first
ever introduced into England. There are here
two Deodar cedars, 58 and 65 feet high, which
had quite assumed the character and habit of
cedars of Lebanon; a *Cunninghamia sinensis*,
25 feet high, with a stem 5 feet in circumference; a *Cryptomeria*, 30 feet; a Douglas fir, 70;
an *Abies morinda*, 65; and a superb *Menziesii*, 70. There is also, among a great many other
very rare plants, a *Pinus ponderosa*, the largest
in England, 80 feet high, raised from a seed
sent Mr. Wells in a letter from the lamented
Douglas, and taken by him from a cone shot
down by his rifle. The collection of rhododendrons was very fine, especially the Sikkins in
the house. Back to Tunbridge, to dinner, at 4;
where, taking train at 5.30, reach St. Leonard's
at 6.20 (Victoria Hotel). Expenses at Tunbridge, and carriage,

April 13.—St. Leonard's. Walk about the
town and on the Esplanade, 3 miles long, the

£ s.
8 16

9 18

18 14

finest in Europe. Leave St. Leonard's at 1, reaching Brighton at 3. (Bedford Hotel.) Bill at St. Leonard's, £2 3s.; to Brighton, 17s., . . . £18 14s. 3 0

April 14.—At Brighton. Walk about the town and on the Esplanade; see the Pavilion, built by George IV., in the Oriental style—some of the rooms, the banqueting-hall, and music-room, being most extraordinary.

April 15.—Leave Brighton by train, at 11, for Ford Station, in 40 minutes; where, by fly, in 15 minutes, to Arundel Castle—Duke of Norfolk's—a portion built by Alfred the Great, before the Norman Conquest, being 1,200 years old. In the keep is a subterranean passage, 5 miles long, to Emberley Castle. Here is a beautiful funebral cypress. The dairy is very pretty and complete, 25 cows being milked by two men and a boy, and the milk and butter cared for by one woman and a girl. Lunch at Ford Station, and at 2.20 by train to Chichester in 20 minutes. (The Dolphin.) Taking a fly, drive 3 miles, to Goodwood, the Duke of Richmond's; an uninteresting house outside, but with some fine rooms and pictures; a most extensive park and race-course; some old cedars and evergreen-oaks. Back to Chichester, to dine, at 6. Bill at Brighton, £9 10s.; fare to Chichester, £1 6s., ... 10 16

April 16.—Leave Chichester at 11, reaching Portsmouth at 11.40. Taking a fly, drive round the town, as also Portsea and Southsea; seeing the dock-yard, where 9,000 men are employed, 32 10 and seeing the Victory, on board of which Lord Nelson was killed, at the battle of Trafalgar. Cab and lunch, 12s.; bill at Chichester, £1 12s.,   £ 32 s. 10

  2   4

April 17.—At 1.10, by boat to Ryde, 6 miles, passing Spithead. Taking carriage after lunch at Ryde, drive 9 miles to the beautiful little village of Shanklin (Daish Hotel).

April 18.—Taking carriage, drive to Appeldercombe; home by Ventnor and Bonchurch, 15 miles. Bill at Shanklin, ...   5 10

April 20.—Leave Shanklin at 11; stopping an hour at Sandrock Hotel, one of the most charming of rural inns, covered with ivy; and later at Northcourt, Sir Henry Gordon's, with a pretty old park of only 15 acres. Lunch at Brixton, where there is an interesting old church 800 years old, where the late Bishop of Oxford was incumbent ten years, and reaching Freshwater about 5, to dine and sleep.

April 21.—Leave Freshwater at 10, passing Farringford House, the residence of Alfred Tennyson; reaching Alum Bay at 11.30 to lunch, after which, taking a boat, row around the Needles, passing through the Camel's Eye into Scratchel's Bay, under immense chalk-cliffs, perfectly white, and 600 feet high; into the great cave, 296 feet long, with the overhanging arch, resplendent with exquisite prismatic colors, and covered with thousands of birds. Returning to Alum Bay, resume carriage, and passing through several lovely villages, including Yarmouth, and Carisbrook with   40 4

its castle and well, to Newport, whence by rail five miles to West Cowes (Fountain). Carriage round the island, ...
Bill at Freshwater, ...

	£	s.
	40	4
	5	16
	2	15

April 22.—Take boat across the Medina River to East Cowes. Seeing the entrance to Osborne, and walking through the grounds of East Cowes Castle; again taking boat, row round end of the island; a superb sea-wall here, belonging to Mr. Bell, of *Bell's Life in London*, costing £30,000. After landing, walk through the town to the Esplanade and Royal Yacht Club House, at 5; take steamer for Southampton at 6. Bill at Cowes, £1 17; boat, etc., 8s., ... 2 5

Southampton (The Dolphin).

April 23.—Leave Southampton by train at 11.35, reaching Oxford (The Mitre), *via* Basingstoke and Reading, at 3.05.

April 24.—Walk through the various colleges and their gardens—the avenue in Christ-Church meadows, and Addison Water-walk, as well as the Botanic Garden, being particularly fine. See the rowing on the river every evening.

April 25.—Taking a carriage, drive eight miles to Blenheim—Duke of Marlborough's—erected in 1707 from designs by Sir John Vanbrugh. It is, perhaps, the finest private palace in England. The suite of state apartments, 400 feet long, is very grand, and filled with magnificent pictures by Rubens, Vandyck, Sir

51 0

Godfrey Kneller, Sir Joshua Reynolds, etc.; that of Sarah, first Duchess of Marlborough, represents her as one of the most beautiful women of that period. The hall is very grand, 67 feet high, and the library, 183 feet long, containing 17,000 volumes, worth £60,000. The gardens also are very fine—some 300 acres, of which 150, in grass, are cut every eight days. Fine masses of rhododendron and one mass of Portugal laurel 320 feet in circumference; the artificial water here is 150 acres. In an enclosure near the garden are shown some emeus, a species of ostrich, which are quite domesticated, breeding every year. The hen lays the eggs, wherever the fancy takes her; the cock gathers them together, and sits upon them himself nine weeks. Lunch at the inn at Woodstock, famous for its gloves, and back to Oxford to dine. Expense, ...   £ s. 51 0   1 5

April 26.—Oxford in the morning. Taking train at 4.15 P. M., reach Buckingham at 6 (Swan and Castle). Bill at Oxford, £10; Oxford to Buckingham, 8s., ...   10 8

April 27.—Walk or drive to Stowe, the magnificent seat of the Duke of Buckingham; the entrance near the hotel, through a grand arch and an avenue, four miles long, of beeches; the house very superb, 969 feet front, and the park very majestic. Lunch at Buckingham, and, taking train at 1.20, reach Woburn (Bedford Arms) at 3.10.

April 28.—Walk to Woburn Abbey, Duke   62 13

	£	s.

of Bedford's, close to the inn; take it all in all, as fine as any place in England—the farm arrangements most extensive and admirable; the house and park superb; and the place wonderfully well kept up. The interior of Woburn Abbey combines more of elegance and comfort than most of the show-houses, the rooms generally not being very large or high, though very ornate. One apartment contains fourteen Vandycks; another was filled with Canalettas, the most valuable collection in the country. In the library—a charming room in white and gold, with windows opening upon the flower-garden, and divided into three parts by columns, with 14,000 volumes—is the original Lion's Mouth, mentioned by Addison in the *Rambler*, into which the contributions to the *Spectator* were thrown. The picture-gallery, 130 feet in length, as well as the different corridors, is filled with splendid pictures of the Bedford family, by Kneller, Lely, Sir Joshua Reynolds, etc.; also some beautiful pictures by Stuart-Newton and Leslie. Here also is the cane which Charles I. left on his last visit here. In a circular room at the end are Canova's Three Graces. The gardens and ornamental grounds—50 acres—are most charmingly laid out and planted—an avenue of araucarias, fifteen years old and some 18 feet high; also one of Deodars, 30 feet high. There is a horse-chestnut here, near the house, though outside the Ha-Ha, 300 feet

62 13

62 13

	£	s.
	62	13

in circumference. An arcade leading from the house through the gardens is one-fifth of a mile long. There is a great deal of ornamental water in park and gardens, mostly formed by the drainage. The park consists of 3,800 acres, filled with deer and sheep, and renowned for its verdure and fertility. The farm-buildings are also very perfect, one large yard, enclosed by a high brick wall, being devoted to different shops—carpenters, painters, joiners—all the houses, carts, fences, buildings, etc., being made on the place, even to repairs to the abbey.

April 29.—Leave Woburn by carriage at 10, driving seven miles to Amphill Park—Lord Wenslydale—a fine old place with a charming avenue; from here, five miles to Wrest Park, Lady Cowper's, a fine house in style of the palace of the Tuileries, with gardens truly royal, like Versailles, with grand water-squares, surrounded by immense yew-hedges and extended vistas of elm, lime, and beech, with statues and temples at the end of the views. The vegetable gardens and training of the fruit-trees most perfect; fifty acres of pleasure-grounds; the walks in the Italian gardens 25 feet wide, and the water-glades and vistas twice this. The American garden was surrounded by a double yew-hedge, a yard or so apart—one, two feet high, the other, three, to represent a lady's flounce; the beds of rhododendrons and azalias being raised from the

	62	13

ground-level to six feet in the centre. From here five miles to station, where take train to Cambridge (The Bull). Bill at Woburn, £2 10s.; fly, £2; train, 18s., ... £ s.
 62 13
  5 8

April 30.—Taking a guide, visit Sydney College, seeing the apartments occupied by Cromwell when a student here, 1616, his name being entered on the college books: "Oliverus Cromwell, Huntingtoniensis, admissus ad commeatum sociorum Aprilis vicissimo sexto, tutore magistro Ricardo Howlett." Over this is written, "Grandis impostor, carnifex perditissimus." To Christ College, seeing the mulberry-tree planted by Milton in 1673; and St. John's College, seeing the chapel, library, and kitchen; also the chapel, library, and kitchen of Trinity, where they daily dine 600 undergraduates; after which, to the Fitzwilliam Museum and Pembroke College, holding only 44 undergraduates; and lastly, to Corpus, Peterhouse, King's, and Queen's. The chapel at King's said to be the finest in Christendom, commenced by Edward IV., and built by different kings to Henry VIII., Richard III. having contributed £700 toward it. Walk through the beautiful grounds of King's, Caius, Clare, and St. John's, down to the boating-station.

May 2.—Leave Cambridge by train at 1.30; reach Audley End, the magnificent seat of Lord Braybrook, a splendid estate given by Henry VIII. to the first Lord Cornwallis, containing one of the grandest of halls and dining- 68 1 rooms; the house, once a Benedictine monastery. A mile beyond is Saffron Walden, where the church is said to be the finest parish church in England. Back to Cambridge at 5.30. Expense, ...

£ s.
68 1

1 0

May 3.—Leave Cambridge at 1.30 by train for Ely (The Lamb), 16 miles, arriving at 2. See the cathedral, by far the most ornate of all the English cathedrals; the wood carvings over the stalls most beautiful; fifteen to twenty subjects from the Old, and as many from the New Testament. The Reredos of alabaster wonderfully carved and enriched with precious stones, at a cost of £3,000. Bill at Cambridge,

9 16

May 4.—Leave Ely at 10.48, reaching King's Lynn (The Globe) at 11.55. After lunch at 1, taking a carriage, drive to Sandringham, 8 miles; seat of the Prince of Wales; an inferior house (in 1866), but a grand, new, and spacious kitchen-garden of fifteen acres—seven within, and eight without the walls. The trees beautifully trained, the pears (Standards) being all trained as distaffs. There are some eight or ten new fruit and forcing houses here, thirty or forty feet long each, four or five of which were devoted to pines, three hundred a year being fruited. Flowers, asparagus, mushrooms, lettuce, beans, peas, and other vegetables, were sent to London every day for the prince's table. The gates of wrought iron to the avenue were very grand, costing £1,600, and given to the prince by the city of Norwich. The interior

78 17

of the house very simple and small, not as large or fine as many country-houses on the Hudson River; the dining-room only holding twenty; the equerries having to be quartered in a cottage, and the servants in the village. The nursery of the future King of England was not over 12 × 15, and his bed a simple little plain cot. A very interesting thing at Sandringham is the method of breeding and raising pheasants. Thirty compartments were each occupied by one cock and twelve hen-pheasants. Every morning the eggs are gathered and placed under common hens, twelve to fifteen to each. When hatched, the hen and young pheasants are removed to coops, each with a little yard. When sufficiently old, the young pheasants are turned out into the preserves. Three thousand are raised in this manner in a single spring. The dog-kennels are likewise well worth seeing, though only for shooting-dogs—pointers, setters, retrievers, etc.

May 5.—Leave the hotel in a carriage at 10, driving first to Houghton House, Lord Cholmondeley's, built by Sir Robert Walpole in 1730; certainly the most superb interior in England. The grand hall, a cube of forty feet, is unsurpassed, the entire sides and ceiling being of elaborately-carved stone, the figures of the size of life. The grand banqueting-room, drawing-rooms, state bedrooms, etc., wonderfully beautiful—especially the ceilings, exquisitely carved, enriched, and gilt; the

£ s.
78 17

78 17

great wonder of the house being the doors of solid mahogany in the state-rooms, highly gilded. The views from the windows of the grand avenues and the park are superb. From here 14 miles on to Holkham, seat of the Earl of Leicester, whose ancestor, Mr. Coke, was considered the first farmer in the country. A grand house and park, with most stately avenues. Back 26 miles to Lynn, making a drive of 52 miles. Bill at Lynn and carriage, . .	£ s. 78 17 9 19

May 6.—Leave Lynn at 1.30 by train, reaching Peterborough (The Angel) at 3.30. Visit the cathedral, a portion of the front being very beautiful; the interior also very handsome, especially the roof of the Lady Chapel. Here is a monument to Mary, Queen of Scots, and Catharine of Arragon, who are buried here, and a stone carved in figures as a memento of the Christians killed by the Danes in 870—a thousand years old. Fare to Peterborough, £1 3s.; bill, £2 6s., ...   3 9

May 7.—Walk or drive to Milton Abbey, Lord Fitzwilliam's, 4 miles from Peterborough. A fine old mansion, time of Henry VIII.; grand old trees in the park, especially one group of horse-chestnuts. Taking train at 5.30, reach Stamford (The George) at 6. Bill at Peterborough, ...   2 6

May 8.—Walk to Burleigh House, Marquis of Exeter's, built and planted by the great Lord Burleigh, Queen Elizabeth's High Treasurer, who (the queen) planted the great elm   94 11

near the house. The hall wonderfully fine, and so are all the state-rooms, which have been occupied by Queen Elizabeth and by Queen Victoria. The original kitchen of Lord Burleigh is still used. The collection of pictures very beautiful. Returning to hotel, take a carriage and drive 25 miles to Kettering (The Royal), passing, first, Deen Park, Lord Cardigan's, the leader of the celebrated charge of the Light Brigade at Balaklava. Deen Park has very beautiful grounds and lake; the Deodar cedars are especially beautiful. From here to Farming Woods, a charming, quaint old place; also with a river, and a superb double avenue. Four miles beyond, Boughton Park, Duke of Buccleugh's, an immense old house, the grounds interspersed with water-glades and avenues, extending in all 76 miles. An ancestor to the present duke was anxious to make an avenue from Boughton to London, 76 miles, but, not being able to accomplish this, he made the same amount of miles in avenue on his own place. Reach Kettering to dinner at 7 o'clock. Bill at Stamford and posting expenses, ...   £ s.
  94 11

  3 00

May 9.—Leave Kettering in posting-carriage at 10 for Rushton Hall, a grand old Elizabethan house, with superb great-timbered hall, where Father Oldcorn and two of the Guy Fawkes conspirators were concealed in the chimney, the place then belonging to Tresham. Taking rail, reach Northampton *via* Wellingborough   97 11

	£	s.

at 12.30. After lunch at the George, take carriage and drive 6 miles to Althorp, Lord Spencer's, a simple but large house, famous for its pictures, there being one of a boy blowing a light, of inestimable value, and many Rubenses, Vandycks, Lelys, Knellers, etc., etc. A grand library of 45,000 volumes, Dryden being once librarian. Here is a Decameron, costing £2,262, put up at auction at £100, with only two bidders—the Duke of Roxburgh and Earl Spencer: second bid, £120; third, £150; and so on, until, within ten minutes, it ran up to £2,262. Also, a Bible in vellum, printed in gold, four hundred years old, costing £600. Back to Northampton to dine, passing a charming place—Harleston House.   97   11

May 10.—Taking carriage, drive 8 miles to Castle Ashby, Marquis of Northampton's, a large though not fine house, with lovely Italian and terrace gardens; charming park, with stately avenue. Back to Northampton to lunch, when, taking train at 2.20, reach Dunstable, famous for its straw hats and larks; going to the Red Lion Inn, where Charles I. slept the night before the battle of Naseby. Bill and carriage at Northampton, £3 16s.; rail to Dunstable, 8s., ...   4   4

May 11.—Leave Dunstable by train at 9.15 for Hatfield, where walk through the grounds and park of Hatfield House, Marquis of Salisbury's, once occupied by Queen Elizabeth and Charles I.; a quaint old garden, with pleached   101   15 alleys and magnificent oaks. From here by rail to St. Albans, where lunch and see the abbey, built fifteen years after the Conquest. From St. Alban's in fifteen minutes by rail to Harrow-on-the-Hill (The Crown); walk to Harrow School, with its beautiful views; visit the church where are the effigies of Lord Byron and Sir Robert Peel, upon the tablet erected to the memory of their tutor. Expenses at Harrow and carriage, ...

£ s.
101 15

3 15

May 12.—Leave Harrow at 9.30, with post-horses across the country to Windsor (The White Hart) in two hours, 18 miles; a charming drive. After seeing the castle, drive through the long walk (3 miles) to the Royal Lodge (where George IV. once lived) and Cumberland Lodge, to Virginia Water, 8 miles in circumference, though artificial, passing the beautiful Roman ruins erected by George IV., supposed to be over two thousand years old. Back to Windsor through the Great Park.

May 14.—Leave Windsor at 10.30, with posting-carriage for Stoke Pogis Church, where Gray wrote his "Elegy in a Country Church-yard," seeing "that yew-tree's shade" —there is but one; "those rugged elms" being in the Eton play-grounds, some mile or more away, and not in the church-yard, as generally supposed; through the magnificent Burnham beeches by Salt Hill (where Eton Montem was formerly held) to Dropmore, Lady Grenville's, celebrated for its collection of conifers. Here

105 10

is a beautiful cedar-of-Lebanon avenue, fifty years old, and the finest deodars, araucarias, douglasiis, etc., in the country, forty to ninety-five feet high, many planted fifty years since; a mile beyond is Cleivden, Duke of Sutherland's, renowned for its exquisite views and flowers. Here is a cedar of Lebanon, brought from Mount Lebanon by Mr. Disraeli. Back through Windsor Great Park to Windsor, where, taking train at 5, reach London at 6. Bill at Windsor and post-horse, . . .	£ s. 105 10 8 10
	£114 0

THIRD TOUR.

ENGLAND AND WALES.

(For Four Persons.—Two Months.)

June 20.—Leave London at 11.45 by train, reaching Devizes at 3.50 (The Bear). See town, churches, etc.

June 21.—Taking carriage at 10, drive first to Sloperton Cottage, where Tom Moore lived and died. A few miles beyond is Bowood, the second finest place in England, Trentham being the first; home by Bromham Churchyard, where Tom Moore is buried.

June 22.—Leaving Devizes at 10, in carriage, drive a few miles, to Erlstoke Park, the seat of Mr. Watson Taylor; a superb park, with magnificent trees. Return to Devizes by 3.

June 24.—Taking posting-carriage at 9, drive through Trowbridge and Westbury, to Warminster, 19 miles; arriving at 12, and lunching at the Bath Arms. Taking a second carriage and fresh horses, drive 5 miles, to Longleat, the magnificent seat of the Marquis of Bath. The park, 30 miles in circumference, 1,000 deer, thirteen or fourteen villages, and half of Frome and Warminster. The house, built 300 years ago by Inigo Jones; the great avenue is particularly grand here. Return to Warminster, to dine. After which, leaving the inn with the first set of horses, reach Devizes at 8.40, 50 miles' drive all round. London to Devizes, £5; expenses at Warminster, £2 10s., . . . 7 10

June 25.—Leaving Devizes at 10, in posting-carriage, drive 14 miles to Marlborough; then with fresh horses, 6 miles, to Savenack—the Marquis of Ailsbury's. Eight immense avenues of beech-trees, converging to a centre, Savenack Forest being the only one in England owned by a subject. Some of the trees here are as fine as in Sherwood Forest. Back to Marlborough, to dine at the Ailsbury Arms. Leaving Marlborough at 6, with the first horses, reach Devizes at 9. Horses and dinner at Marlborough, ... 1 18

June 26.—Visit Devizes Castle, near the hotel, first built in 1107; destroyed by Cromwell; rebuilt by Mr. Leach, who has restored it most wonderfully; with beautiful grounds. At 2 take train for Bristol, and by carriage to Clifton—Clifton Downs Hotel—by 4. See Suspension-bridge, 700 feet long, 230 feet high, and 34 feet wide. Bill at Devizes and horses, one week, 19 9

June 28.—Walk about the town and rocks. After lunch drive in carriage to Blaize Castle and the Henbury Cottages, most charmingly 28 17

	£	s.

designed and arranged for the poor people of the estate; also Henbury Church, . . .   28   17

June 29.—Leave Clifton at 12.45, reaching Chepstow at 2.30. Walk to Chepstow Castle, where Henry Martyn, one of the regicides, was confined 20 years. Bill at Clifton, 5 days, £15; rail to Chepstow, £1, ...   16   0

June 30.—Walk or drive 3 miles, to Piercefield Park, with fine views. After lunch drive in carriage, 5 miles, to Tintern Abbey (Beaufort Arms). Bill at Chepstow and carriage, 3 days,   9   15

July 1.—Walk or drive to Wyndclyff. Beautiful view of the Wye; and back to the Abbey rest of the day.

July 2.—Leaving Tintern in a carriage with post-horses at 9.30, reach Monmouth at 12. Lunch at Beaufort Arms; after which drive to Troy House, an old place of the Duke of Beaufort's. Seeing Henry V.'s cradle and a famous old mantelpiece. Home by Colefort and by Clearwell Court, seat of the Countess of Dunraven, a fine old castellated house of the sixteenth century, with a most charming little church. Back to Tintern by 8. Expenses, .   2   10

July 6.—Leave Tintern at 10 in carriage with post-horses, for Raglan, where lunch; after which walk to Raglan Castle, perhaps the finest ruin in England. Back to Tintern by 8. Expenses, ...   2   10

July 11.—Bill at Tintern, 8 days, . .   16   13

Leaving Tintern at 12, in carriage, drive 5 miles, ...   76   5 to Chepstow; then by rail through Cardiff, Neathe, Newport, etc., to Carmarthen (The Ivy-Bush), at 6; 96 miles. Expenses of rail, . . £ s. 76 5 / 4 16

July 12—Leaving the inn at 10, drive in carriage and post-horses through the lovely vale of Towy, passing Abergwili, with the palace of the Bishop of St. Davids; Grongar Hill, the subject of Dyer's beautiful poem; the ruins of Dryslynn Castle, wonderfully situated on a conical hill; Dynevor Castle, Lord Dynevor's, a magnificent park, with majestic masses of oaks, a fine house, and lovely flower-garden; to Landlilo, where lunch, at the Cawdor Arms. Starting again at 3, reach in half an hour Golden Grove, Earl of Cawdor's, a grand castellated house, having a front, including stables and offices, of nearly 500 feet, with most exquisitely-kept pleasure-grounds. The collection of the new evergreens very large and very perfect in shape by means of the shears. The view from the terrace very extensive and beautiful, resembling that from Windsor Castle; embracing, among other things, three ruined castles. Passing a mile or so beyond, Middleton Park, Sir William Paxton's, and Ty Gwyn, once the residence of Sir Richard Steele, where he wrote "The Conscious Lovers," and much of the *Spectator*, *Tatler*, and *Rambler*. Back to the Ivy-Bush, where Steele died—about 30 miles.

July 13.—Bill at Carmarthen, £4 12s.; carriage, £2, ... 6 12

Leave at 1 by train, reaching Tenby (White

87 13

	£	s.
Lion) at 2; a charmingly-situated little Welsh watering-place. Walk about the town and sands. Rail from Carmarthen,	87	13
	1	6

July 14.—Leave Tenby at 10, with post-horses; driving 5 miles, to Manorbeer Castle, a fine old ruin; then 2 miles farther, to Lamphey, an old ruined palace of the Bishops of St. Davids, with an exquisite mullioned window; and 2 miles beyond, to Pembroke, where lunch. After which, 5 miles, to Stackpole Court, another seat of the Earl of Cawdor's; 2 miles beyond this, St. Govan's Chapel, in a most desolate fissure in the rocks, once inhabited by a hermit; 2 miles farther is the Huntsman's Leap and the Caldron or Punch-bowl, an extraordinary hole, 200 to 300 feet deep, with the sea flowing in and out; 2 miles again beyond this you come to the Stacks, three wonderful rocks, rising one hundred or more feet from the sea, and covered with myriads of a peculiar sea-bird, which from time immemorial come here, from Russia, to breed. Ten miles back to Pembroke, to dine, and see the castle. Leaving Pembroke at 8 P.M., reach Tenby at 9.30. A very delightful excursion of 46 miles (all round). Dinner at Pembroke, £1; carriage and driver, £1 16s., ... 2 16

July 18.—Bill at Tenby, 6 days, . . . 15 0
Leave Tenby at 11.30 for Carmarthen, . . 1 15
Carmarthen to Strada Florida, rail, . . . 1 0

109 10

	£	s.
Thence by carriage (1867)—rail probably now finished—to Aberystwith at 6 P. M. (Bellevue Hotel), ...	109	10
		16
Bill at Aberystwith, one week, . . .	15	0

July 24.—Leaving Aberystwith at 1.05, by train, reach Shrewsbury at 5 (The Raven Inn). A very beautiful journey through a lovely valley. Shrewsbury, a very quaint old town, with a very beautiful walk called "The Quarry."

| Bill at Shrewsbury, ... | 4 | 10 |

July 25.—Leave Shrewsbury at 2.45, by train, reaching Oswestry (Wynstay Arms), an old-fashioned inn, with a bowling-green.

July 26.—Walk or drive 2 miles, to Pokington Park, a fine place, with a superb cedar of Lebanon. At 1, in carriage and post-horses, to Brinkinalt, a fine, well-kept place and charming house, belonging to Lord E. Hill, and where the Duke of Wellington used to stay when a boy. After this to Chirk Castle, seat of Colonel Biddulph, founded in 1013, but battered down by Cromwell. In one of the chambers is the bed used by Charles I., and a beautiful cabinet given the family by the king. The quadrangle of the castle is very fine, with Elizabethan windows; and all the old apartments are in admirable keeping and preservation. Most superb views into 17 counties. Back by 6 to Oswestry.

July 27.—Walk or drive 1½ miles, to Park Hall, perhaps the most extraordinary and ancient old-timbered house in the country; a   129 16 very curious old hall, in oak, with a black oaken table, to dine 25, 20 feet long, by 6 to 8 feet wide, made, in 1583, of one plank. The drawing-room, dining-room, corridor (with old family portraits) all panelled in dark oak, with heavy carved bedsteads and chairs; and an estate of 500 acres. The small diamond windows in great bays, extending the whole width of the different projections, were very curious; the house being on three sides of a square, with a quaint old terrace. From here to an old ruined castle, very picturesque, and beautifully situated, belonging to the De Warrens. Near by an old village, Wittington, with its old houses, and church covered with religious mottoes. Home by Aston Park, to dine. Bill at Oswestry, 3 days, and 2 carriages, ... £129 16s / 8 15

July 28.—Leave Oswestry by rail at 10.40, reaching Llangollen at 12.15 (The Hand). Walk about the town, seeing the curious old carved house of the Ladies of Llangollen—Lady Emily Butler and Miss Ponsonby—who lived here together in male costume for forty-odd years. Rail, ... 1 18

Aug. 1.—Walk by the banks of the canal to Valle Crucis Abbey, a beautiful ruin quite equal in parts to Tintern. After lunch, drive to Wynstay, residence of Sir William Watkins Wynn, a fine old park with a grand avenue and new house in the French chateau style, the old house, with valuable library and pictures,

140 9

	£	s.

having been burnt in 1858. Walk to the old castle Dinas, on top of the mountain opposite the hotel. Bill at Llangollen, three days, . . . 140 9

Aug. 2.—Leaving Llangollen at 12, reach Shrewsbury at 1.40, and the quaint old town of Ludlow (The Feathers—most picturesque of inns) at 2.30. Rail, ... 2 5

After lunch, walk to Ludlow Castle, a splendid old ruin, though admirably well preserved, most interesting as having been the residence of Edward, Prince of Wales, after his marriage with Catharine of Arragon, subsequently queen of Henry VIII.; also of the young princes who later were smothered in the tower by their uncle, Richard III. Here, too, Milton wrote his "Comus," which was performed before the court. Over the gate Butler lived, and wrote his "Hudibras." Sir Henry Sydney, father of the famous Sir Philip Sydney, was governor here under Queen Elizabeth. Take it all in all, Ludlow Castle is as interesting a ruin as any in England, from its admirable preservation and the great number of historical characters and events connected with it.

Aug. 3.—Taking a carriage at 10.30, drive through the lovely village of Broomfield to Downton Castle, the residence of the late celebrated horticulturist, Andrew Knight, for many years the president of the London Horticultural Society—a beautiful house, charming flower-garden, grand views over a magnificent park. From here to Oakley Park—Lady Mary 150 13

Clive's; superb trees, and a great estate—all the eye embraced from the house; by Comus Valley and Haywood, where the scene of the "Masque" was laid, and where George Barnwell, the London apprentice, killed his uncle. Home by Moor Park, a fine old place two miles from Ludlow. Carriage, ...   £ s.
150 13

1 10

Aug. 4.—Drive again, or walk, to Oakley Park, to see the Druid oaks, said to be 3,000 years old. From here to Downton Hall, Sir Charles Boughton's; beautiful lawn and flower-gardens, and fine extensive views. Bill at Ludlow, three days, and carriage, . . .   5 10

Aug. 5.—Leave Ludlow at 10.30, and, after three changes, reach Kidderminster at 1.10. After lunch at The Lion, drive to Hagley Hall, seat of Lord Lyttleton (Coke on Lyttleton), fine house and grand park; and to Leasowes, the home of the poet Shenstone.

Aug. 6.—Leaving Kidderminster at 11, drive to Stewart Castle, Colonel Foster's, celebrated for the perfection of his stables, eight hunters being kept here, each in a separate box, well ventilated, and heated in winter by hot-water pipes. The saddle-and-harness rooms in most admirable condition—the bits, stirrups, chains, etc., polished as bright as silver. Eighteen horses are kept here, one man for every two horses. From here a few miles beyond to Enville Hall, Earl of Stamford and Warrington's, *the finest ornamental grounds in the world:*

157 13

75 acres of mown lawn; a splendid conservatory, costing £18,000; four lakes; a purple beech, 350 feet in circumference (the branches); some horse-chestnuts and limes even larger; a pinus nobilis, 50 feet high; taxodium distichum, perhaps 100 feet in circumference on the ground; a Douglas fir, 100 feet high; and endless specimens of cedars of Lebanon, deodars and araucarias. Back to Kidderminster by Lea Castle, a charming place, well kept, fine trees and grounds.

	£	s.
	157	13

Aug. 7.—Leave Kidderminster at 11 in posting-carriage, 11 miles, for Whitby Court, Lord Dudley and Ward's. The whole effect of the place very stately, Lord Dudley having spent within a few years £400,000 upon it. The lake is not as fine as that at Trentham. The house, a mixture of Trentham and Bowood, is very grand; the church also very beautiful. The estate here runs 12 miles on each side. The farms are in exceedingly good condition—rented at from 30s. to £2 10s. an acre, and the farmer may double and treble his rent, as each acre usually produces, when well cultivated, from 15 to 25 bushels of wheat. Bill, three days at Kidderminster, and three carriages, ... 12 0

Aug. 8.—Leave Kidderminster at 9.05 by train, reaching Oxford (King's Head) at 1. Rail, Kidderminster to Oxford, . . . 2 5
See colleges (before described).

171 18

	£	s.

Aug. 9.—Leave Oxford by train, reaching Dorking (Red Lion) at 4.20. Bill at Oxford, £2 10; rail to Dorking, £2 10, . . . | 171 18 | |
| 5 | 0 |

Aug. 10.—Walk to Deepdeen, the residence of Mr. Hope, the author of "Anastasius," and where Disraeli wrote "Coningsby"—a most beautiful place, and in admirable keeping; 14 acres of dressed ground, and 14 men and 2 boys allowed for the gardens and houses—yet the place has never cost over £800 a year. Few places in England have more artistic beauty than Deepdeen.

Aug. 11.—Drive to the Rookery, a quaint old place with terraced flower-garden over a pretty lake; next to Walton Hall, where Evelyn, author of the celebrated "Sylva," was born and died; thence to Abinger Hall—Lord Abinger's—a cosy, homeish place, and back by Denbies, a grand mansion on a high hill.

Aug. 12.—The Lion Inn at Dorking once belonged to Cardinal Wolsey, and the principal parlor, though covered with paper, is really panelled in oak, and was the cardinal's dining-room. Near The Lion is the old inn described by Dickens in the Pickwick Club as The Marquis of Granby, where old Tony Weller and Brother Stiggins, the shepherd, lived. After lunch, drive to Juniper Hall, with splendid cedars. Here Miss Burney, authoress of "Evelina," resided; afterward to Burford Bridge Inn, where Keats, the poet, passed his honeymoon, and wrote "Endymion;" still farther, by a charm- 176 18

	£	s.
ing drive, through Leatherhead to Pulsden, which the great Sheridan once owned. Back by 5, to dinner. Bill and carriage at Dorking, 6 days, ...	176 16	18 10
Aug. 13.—Leave Dorking at 10.30, reaching London at 11.53. Rail, ...		12
	194	0

NOTE.—This trip could easily be accomplished in 15 to 20 days.

FINEST HOUSES IN ENGLAND: Houghton House, Lord Cholmondeley, near Lynn; Burleigh House, Earl of Exeter, Stamford; Badminton, Duke of Beaufort, Bath; Wentworth House, Earl Fitzwilliam, Rotherham; Castle Howard, Earl of Carlisle, Scarborough; Blenheim, Duke of Marlborough, Oxford; Chatsworth, Duke of Devonshire, Matlock.

FINEST PLACES IN ENGLAND: Trentham, Duke of Sutherland, Stoke; Bowood, Marquis of Lansdowne, Chippingham; Blenheim, Duke of Marlborough, Oxford; Enville, Lord Stamford and Warrington, near Kidderminster (best flower-garden in England).

MOST INTERESTING PLACES: Knole, Lord Amherst, Tunbridge; Penshurst, Lord De Lisle, Tunbridge; Haddon Hall, Duke of Rutland, Matlock.

BEST COLLECTION OF TREES: Highnam Court, Gambia Parry, near Gloucester; Redleaf, William Wells, Tunbridge; Deepdeen, Mr. Hope, Dorking; Dropmore, Lady Grenville, Windsor.

ENGLAND.

Most Remarkable Places: Levens Hall, Mrs. Hamilton, Boness; Biddulph Grange, Mr. Bateman, Congleton; Alton Towers, Lord Shrewsbury, Congleton; Studley Royal, Earl De Grey and Ripon (Fountain's Abbey), Ripon; Elvaston Castle, Earl of Harrington, Derby.

Finest Castles: Windsor; Warwick; Belvoir; Alnwick; Arundel.

Finest Ruins: Ludlow Castle; Raglan Castle; Pembroke Castle; Tintern Abbey; Fountain Abbey; Melrose Abbey.

FOURTH TOUR.

FROM LONDON, THROUGH BELGIUM, HOLLAND, DENMARK, NORWAY, SWEDEN, RUSSIA, POLAND, AND PRUSSIA, TO PARIS.

June 6.—Leave London by steamer at 5 A. M. from St. Catharine's Docks for Ostend, reaching Ostend at 4 P. M.; or from London to Dover by rail, thence by steamer to Ostend. Taking rail at 5.30, reach Bruges at 6.10 (Hotel du Commerce). Expenses, £6 10s.

June 7.—Taking a valet de place, see the principal churches, cathedral, Hôtel de Ville, etc. Leaving Bruges at 12.30 by rail, reach Ghent (Royal) at 1.45; after lunch, see the cathedral, with its wonderful picture by the brothers Ten Eyck (for which the King of Prussia offered two million francs), and the convent of the Beguines, where there are nine hundred nuns.

June 8.—Leave Ghent by rail at 9.15, reaching Antwerp (St. Antoine) at 10.30. See the cathedral, with Rubens's celebrated picture of the "Descent from the Cross," and the "Marriage of St. Catharine;" also the museum and other churches, famous for their pulpits.

June 9.—Leave Antwerp by rail at 10 for Rotterdam—two hours by rail and two hours by boat, passing Dort, a very picturesque old Dutch town, and arriving at Rotterdam at 3. Drive about the town for an hour; then, taking rail at 4, reach the Hague (Bellevue) in forty minutes.

June 10.—Drive about the town and to the museum, to see the gallery. Leave the Hague at 2 by rail, reaching Amsterdam at 4 (Dolan Hotel); see the town, churches, etc.

June 11.—By steamer to Brock and back, after which visit the pictures at the Musée, and the palace, as well as Mr. Hope's collection. At the palace is the largest hall in Europe, one hundred feet high, without a support.

June 12.—Leave Amsterdam at 8.20 A. M. by rail, reaching Dusseldorf at 2; see the pictures, Hopgarten, and Prince Frederick's palace (Hotel Breidenbocker Hof).

June 13.—Leave Dusseldorf at 8 by train, reaching Hanover at 2. Drive through the old parts of the town, to the beautifully-carved old house of Leibnitz, and to the museum, with many interesting pictures, and through a fine old avenue of limes to the king's summer palace. At Hanover, Royal Hotel.

June 14.—Leave Hanover at 9 by rail, reaching Harburg at 1.30, and Hamburg (Streit's hotel) by carriage at 3. See town, water-square, Jew quarter, etc.

NOTE.—The above trip through Belgium and Holland is, of course, very brief and imperfect, but may be made as much longer as necessary. It is only mentioned incidentally here, as being *en route* to the north of Europe.

June 19.—Leave Hamburg at 10 A. M., reaching Altona at 10.30, and Kiel at 2.30, where dine and remain until 8 P. M., when, taking steamer, reach Korsöe at 2 A. M. Leaving Korsöe at 7 A. M. by rail, reach Copenhagen (Royal Hotel) at 10.30; visit Thorwaldsen's Museum, palace and gardens of Fredericksburg, with fine views from terrace.

June 20.—Drive to the celebrated Deer Park, as fine in sylvan effects and grouping of trees—principally beeches—as any thing in England; superb single trees and beautiful glades and woods; lunch at a gardenhouse in the forest, and drive home at 6, by the strand, with pretty villas and gardens overlooking the Swedish coast.

June 21.—Walk to Rosenburg Gardens and about the town.

June 22.—Leave Copenhagen in steamer at 12, passing Elsinore, and reaching Gottenburg about midnight, stopping an hour to land and take in passengers.

June 23.—Still at sea, but about 3 pass into Christiania Fiord, the entrance to which, as well as the first approach to Christiania, is very striking, though the general course of the Fiord is not unlike the Hudson through the highlands; reach Christiania in broad daylight at 11 P. M. (Victoria Hotel).

NOTE.—The author cannot too strongly recommend all travellers intending to make the tour through Norway, to consult Mr. T. Bennett, No. 17, Store Strandgade, Christiania. Mr. Bennett, who is a most courteous, amiable, and educated gentleman, and has been acting English vice-consul in Norway for many years, can give every traveller all the advice and counsel necessary for his comfort, being himself the author of a most excellent guide-book through this country, and is prepared to furnish money, carrioles, and every thing necessary for a successful journey. One of the essentials in Norway is a complete suit of water-proof clothes and hat, and an india-rubber cloth to protect the luggage from hard rain, to which, in open carrioles, one is constantly exposed. One should never be without a bottle or so of brandy, and a moderate amount of biscuit and canned meat, which can be procured at Christiania, and still better at Trondhjem, and which are most valuable at inferior stations. As a general rule, you find at all stations excellent beer, good coffee, and generally fresh salmon, but often nothing else.

June 24.—Walk or drive about the town, and to Oscarhalle, with beautiful pictures and views.

July 4.—Leave Christiania (four persons and two servants) at 12 by rail to Eishalt, two and a half hours; then by boat to Lilliehammer, on the Miösen Lake, arriving at 10 P. M., broad daylight (Mrs. Ormsrud's Hotel). Bill at Christiania, one week, and five carriages, £20.

July 5.—Leave Lilliehammer in open carriage and three horses at 7 A. M., and a car and one horse with the luggage; having a most wonderful drive up the Gudbransdalen valley—immense mountains on either side, with the rapid river Logan running through. After 28 miles' posting, stop at Skjeggestad to dine at 1. Leaving again at 3, reach Viig at 8 P. M. to sleep.

Charmingly situated, the river making a great bend round the house, backed by superb mountains, with snow-capped tops.

July 6.—Leave Viig at 7.30, passing through magnificent but very wild and gloomy scenery, and by some wretched huts; reach Brœmhaugen to dine at 1. Leaving here at 3, reach Jerkin in the Dovrefield to sleep, at 10.30 P. M. The last 20 miles above vegetation, meeting numerous reindeer—4,000 feet above the level of the sea, passing between two desolate lakes, and no human habitations of any sort for 15 miles.

July 7.—Leave Jerkin at 3 P. M., passing over an elevation of 4,500 feet, and then descending with great rapidity on a fast trot and even gallop, having fine views of Sneehatten—the highest mountain in Norway, 8,000 feet. From Kongsvold to Drivstuen—a wonderful drive; and scenery in grandeur and sublimity equal to the Alps; a magnificent road the whole distance; reaching Ny-orne-i-opdal at 9—a very clean station, where you get the first white bread and excellent beds.

July 8.—Leave Ny-orne-i-opdal at 7.30, passing a great ravine, 700 to 1,000 feet deep, and a great deal of grand scenery, and reaching Stören, the railway station, at 2, where dine, and, taking rail at 6, reach Trondhjem (Hotel d'Angleterre), the capital of Norway, at 8.40, after a most wonderful land journey in carriages, or carrioles, of 5 days from Christiania.

July 9.—See Trondhjem; the palace and cathedral, where the kings of Norway and Sweden are crowned.

July 11.—Leave Trondhjem at 6 P. M. on steamer

for Hammerfest, the "Nordman" being a very comfortable boat, with good state-rooms and excellent table, though apt to be overcrowded at this season.

July 12.—Arrive at Namsöe about 5 A. M., where the boat stops an hour, and where passengers go ashore to visit the town; rest of the day the steamer passes through wonderful scenery—high, steep mountains, sharp and pointed, with thousands of islands.

July 13.—Pass the line of the Arctic circle about 4 P. M. Scenery equally wonderful to-day; rugged sharp mountains, 1,500 to 2,000 feet high, covered with clouds and snow; quantities of islands, and numerous narrow passages hardly wide enough for the boat to pass. At a distance is Torghatten, 1,000 feet high, with a hole through it; also the Seven Sisters, 4,000 feet high, and Hest Mansöen (Huntsman's Island). About 10 P. M. reach Bodö, where disembark for an hour or so; full daylight, the sun apparently setting about 11 P. M. Great numbers of eider duck in this neighborhood.

July 14.—Snow-capped mountains, occasional narrow passages, and great fiords, all day.

July 15.—Reach Tromsöe about 11 P. M. From a hill near the town, the midnight sun can be seen. Many travellers are satisfied to go no farther north, waiting here a week for the return-boat, which usually remains here several hours, enabling the passengers to walk three miles through deep mud and across roaring torrents to a Lapp settlement, where can be seen about 500 reindeer.

July 16.—At sea all day, passing through fiords; reaching Hammerfest, the most northerly town in the world, at 11 P. M. Taking a boat, row out beyond the projecting headland of the harbor; seeing the *midnight sun*, on this occasion setting about northeast, as low as 20 degrees, or about 4 diameters above the horizon—north declination of the sun, 19° 21'; altitude of centre of sun at midnight, 0° to 1°.

July 17.—At Hammerfest. Ascend the Thief Fjeld, 2,000 feet high. From here the view extends beyond the North Cape, embracing over 60 lakes and fiords; at midnight the full sunlight. Return to steamer on your downward passage.

July 18.—Wild, precipitous scenery all day—mountains covered with snow, in some instances to the water's edge with glaciers. Great numbers of eider duck, which are said to be such good sitters as never to abandon their nests, even when a rock is blasted near them.

July 19 *to* 24.—At sea, running through fiords and narrow passages, and finally reaching Trondhjem again, at 9 P. M., after 14 days' steaming (Hôtel d'Angleterre.)

July 20 *to* 26.—At Trondhjem.

July 27.—Leave Trondhjem at 5 P. M., in steamer, arriving at Christiansund early on morning of 28th July; where go ashore, the boat remaining here two hours.

July 28.—The town very peculiarly situated on rocks around a circle of water, with one very narrow entrance like a canal. Reach Molde about 1, beautifully situated on a fiord; see the Leper's hospital.

July 29.—Leave Molde at 9 A. M. in a small steamer; down the Molde Fiord, very beautiful, especially the lower part, which is wonderful. Reaching Veblungsnæssett at 1; where, taking carrioles, drive to Aak, most splendidly situated under the Romsdal Horn, said to be the best station in Norway, except that at Jerkin, on the Dovrefield. Leaving Aak after dinner, at 4.30, in carrioles, drive 30 miles through the celebrated Romsdalen Pass, under perpendicular and jagged mountains, 2,000 to 4,000 feet high, through fearful passes and by numerous water-falls, to Ormein; arriving at 9 o'clock, to sleep.

July 30.—Leave Ormein at 11 in carrioles for Nystuen and back, 14 miles; very fine, with grand falls. In the afternoon, ascend the mountain back of the station at Ormein.

July 31.—Leave Ormein at 8 in carrioles, and, after another wonderful drive through the Romsdalen, reach Aak, to dine, at 1 o'clock.

Aug. 1.—Leave Aak at 1, in carrioles, for Veblungsnæssett, where, taking steamer for Molde, arrive at 7 P. M.

Aug. 3.—Leave Molde in steamer at 1, reaching Aalsund at 5 P. M. Go on shore for an hour; sleeping on board steamer.

Aug. 4.—Reach Bergen at 5. Charmingly situated.

Aug. 5.—See Museum, Athenæum, etc.; German church.

Aug. 7.—Leave Bergen at 8 in steamer, for the Hardanger Fiord; reaching Eide, through grand scenery, at 9 P. M., and sleeping on board steamer.

Aug. 8.—Leave Eide at 3 A. M., passing Ulvic and Vik, at head of the Fiord. At Vik leave the steamer, if you wish to go to the Voringfoss—10 hours' good walking from and back to Vik. On from Vik, through magnificent scenery, passing Utne and the glacier Folgen Fond, to Odde,* and thence back to Eide, to sleep; leaving the steamer at 5 o'clock. An excellent station at Eide.

Aug. 10.—Leave Eide at 10 in carrioles, through wonderful scenery and the grandest zigzag road, to Vossevangen, where dine and sleep. An excellent house here.

Aug. 12.—Leave Vossevangen in carrioles at 9, over a very fine though very hilly road, to Stalheim, where the wonderful descent commences by the zigzag, twelve turns being in sight at once, into the valley of the Nærodal, by far the finest scenery in Norway—truly sublime. Reach Gudvangen at 3, to dine. Opposite the Heilfoss, 2,000 feet high. Taking the steamer in the evening, reach Lærdalsoren at 12, through wonderful scenery.

Aug. 13.—Remain at Lærdalsoren; walk to end of the Fiord, and also in the other direction from the town.

Aug. 14.—Leave Lærdalsoren at 8.30, in carrioles, and, after a wonderful drive, reach Hæg, to lunch; after lunch, pass the old and interesting church of Borgund, built in the eleventh century. The drive the rest of the

---

* Remain here, at Odde, 2 days, if desirous of seeing the Skjieggefoss, the largest fall in the Old World; and also to visit the great iceglacier, Folgefarden, behind Odde. There are also some very interesting water-falls — Lothefossen — and quite a beautiful drive to them. Fast stations. From Odde, by steamer or boat, 14 hours, to Vik, and from there to the Voringfoss and back, 2 days, unless visited before. Utne, 20 English miles above Odde, on the fiord, is an excellent station to stop at.

day runs through a magnificent pass cut in the side of tremendous mountains, bordering beautiful lakes filled with islands. Toward night reach the summit of the Fille Fjeld, 3,170 feet above the sea, but quite as wild and dreary as the Dovrefield. Above all vegetation, except reindeer-moss and heather. Pass several sætors, with herds of cows, sheep, and goats, kept here in the summer, and driven in at night round the fires, to keep off the bears and wolves, which abound here. Many herds of reindeer are or were seen crossing the glaciers in many places. Reach Nystuen, on the summit of the Fille Fjeld, at 6; a poor station, where potted meats are indispensable.

Aug. 15.—Leave Nystuen at 8.30, in carrioles. Another magnificent drive through Skogstad, fearfully wild and grand, and Thune to Oildé; stopping here to lunch. In the afternoon through more magnificent scenery, by the banks of the beautiful Strand Fiord, to Fagernæs, to sup and sleep. An excellent station.

Aug. 16.—Leave Fagernæs at 8.45 in carrioles. A magnificent drive all day; very lofty mountains, and charming views over lakes; especially the Strand Fiord, filled with beautiful islands. Reach Skoien at 5. Good station.

Aug. 17.—Leave Skoien at 6.30 A. M., for steamer on Rands Fiord; driving 2 miles, and leaving in the boat at 8 o'clock, breakfasting on board. Reach the glass-works at end of the lake (50 miles), at 12.30, when in carrioles to Viig, to dine and sleep. Scenery on lake pretty, but tamer than the usual Norwegian scenery.

Aug. 18.—Leave Viig at 9, on horseback, to ascend Krogleven, to the King's and Queen's Views; the former the most exquisite view in Norway. About 11 take carrioles at foot of the mountain, leaving the saddle-horses; and, after a magnificent drive of 3½ Norwegian (25 English) miles, reach Christiania at 4 P. M., after nearly 6 weeks' absence, and a cost, for 4 persons and 2 servants, of $940 in gold.

Aug. 20.—Leave Christiania at 7, in steamer The Excellency Tohl (the best boat), reaching Gottenburg (Gotha Galla Hotel) at midnight.

Aug. 21.—Visit the Botanic Garden—the statues of Gustavus Adolphus and The Rivals, the latter especially fine. Gottenburg is, perhaps, next to Hamburg, the best-built and handsomest town in Northern Europe.

Aug. 22.—Leave Gottenburg at 6 in.canal-boat by the Gotha Canal, the views on the Gotha River being very pretty and picturesque; passing the grim old castle of Bonus, and, by 11, reaching the beautiful falls at Trolhættan, where the boat takes 1½ hours to get up the wonderful locks, at a toll of $250 (silver dollars). These falls, the most considerable in Europe in their way. About 2, pass several locks and pretty scenery and country-houses, a large town—Wernsborg, and soon into the Wener Lake, the largest in Europe, 100 by 50 miles, passing, toward night, into very narrow passages, and so again into the canal, sleeping on board boat.

Aug. 23.—Leave boat at Toraboda at 7 A. M.; breakfasting at railway-station, and taking train at 10.30, reach Stockholm at 5.30 (Rydberg Hotel, one of the best houses in Europe).

NOTE.—The above route is better than either rail or

boat for the entire journey from Gottenburg to Stockholm, as the one day on the Gotha Canal gives you the falls of Trolhættan and the prettiest scenery.

Aug. 24.—See the palace, the interior being as fine as any thing abroad, especially the Dresden China Boudoir, where the mirror-frames, chandeliers, and even chairs, were of china. The private apartments of the king are charming, especially his armory, smoking-room, and antique tankard room, filled with every variety of Scandinavian tankards and drinking-vessels. The Indian and Chinese rooms, atelier, and bedrooms, were very perfect. Visit also the royal stables and church, where are the bodies of Gustavus Vasa and Charles XII. After lunch at 2, by carriage to the country palace of Prince Oscar, at Bellevue. Also, to the charming summer residence of the king at Rosendal, filled with the most quaint and extraordinary things: the Drinkhalle, with 183 cups of delf and glass; another room, with numerous tankards, plates, and chandeliers of engraved *lead*. Back to dine at the celebrated *café* in the Deer Garden.

Aug. 25.—Take steamer, at 11, up the Malar Lake, to Drottingholm (6 miles), or Queen's Island, belonging to the queen-dowager, a splendid palace; one chamber, that of Gustavus Adolphus, of blue and gold, being as ornate and elaborate as it is possible to conceive; the gardens, fountains, clipped trees, and Chinese palace, very fine. Back to Stockholm at 4 P. M.

Aug. 27.—Take steamer at 8 A. M. up the Malar Lake, reaching, about 12, the wonderful old chateau of Skokloster, built, in 1630, by the celebrated Wrangle family, and now in possession of the Brays, the most noble family in Sweden. There is not in Europe a more peculiar or distinctive chateau than this: a large quadrangle, the galleries filled with very curious and quaint old pictures, and on and over the doors are sentences in Latin, Greek, and other languages. The rooms, which are very large and numerous, have extraordinary mantel-pieces of carved and colored wood, and the ceilings with projecting figures as large as life; wonderful old cabinets filled with exquisite glass goblets and tankards taken in the Thirty Years' War. The walls, covered with gobelin tapestry, uncommonly fresh and well preserved. Leaving here by another steamer, reach, in 1½ hours, Upsala, the ancient Scandinavian capital, beautifully situated at the end of a narrow river or canal. The cathedral here, built in 1258, is very fine, equal in size and character to any in England. Beneath the altar is buried Linnæus. The tombs of the great Gustavus Vasa and his two wives are in the Lady Chapel; so, also, the crown of John III. The university, which is scattered about the town, was founded in 1477, and generally contains 1,400 students, all wearing a white cap, and looking like simple, quiet, hard-working young men. Visit the house of Linnæus and his Botanic Garden, having quantities of Norway spruces cut into square blocks. Dine and sleep at Upsala.

Aug. 28.—Leave Upsala at 8, in steamer down the Malar Lake, in which are some 300 islands, reaching Stockholm at 1.30.

Sept. 1.—Leave Stockholm at 2 A. M., in steamer, going on board the night before, for St. Petersburg;

the passage across the Baltic often very rough, until you get among the islands. Reach Abo, in Gulf of Finland, at 5, the first Finnish-Russian town; going ashore for an hour or so, but returning on board steamer to sleep.

Sept. 2.—At sea more or less all day, reaching Viborg at 7 P. M.; ashore for an hour or so; passing several forts to-day, destroyed by the English during the Crimean War.

Sept. 3.—Leaving Viborg early, reach Cronstadt at 3. At 4.30, first view of the golden dome of Isaac's Church and the spire of the Admiralty; reach St. Petersburg at 5.30 (Hotel de Russie—excellent).

Sept. 4.—Drive to the Summer and Winter Palaces, the Nevskoi Prospekt, the fort, and Isaac's Church, which is most magnificent. Outside, the base and columns are of red granite, or porphyry. Inside, one mass of gold, marble, and precious stones; the grand altar being supported by six columns, 50 feet high—four of malachite and two of lapis-lazuli.

Sept. 5.—Taking steamer, go to Peterhoff, seeing the splendid golden statues and fountains, equal to Versailles; the palace and gardens very interesting.

Sept. 6.—Leave St. Petersburg at 2.30 in sleeping-carriage, on rail for Moscow—400 miles—reaching Moscow at 9 next morning (Mme. Billet's Hotel).

Sept. 7.—Taking carriage, drive to the Kremlin, where ascend Ivan's Tower, having a wonderful view of 1,500 churches, with their domes—red, blue, yellow, orange, and green, many of them gilded—one of the most remarkable views in the world for a city. After which, drive round the town for two or three hours, seeing all the palaces, mosques, monasteries, etc., and out to Peterskoi, where Napoleon lived during the conflagration of Moscow.

Sept. 8.—To the Kremlin, to see the various churches, filled with gold, pictures, and precious stones—diamonds, pearls, turquoises—many the size of a shilling. Subsequently, through the vast collection of robes, mitres, etc., for the patriarch and bishops, one mass of the most precious stones, of immense size, though not well polished. Here, also, are great silver and gold vessels (kettles) for making the holy oil. After lunch, drive to the celebrated monastery of Seminoff, 3 miles from Moscow; splendid music; about thirty monks.

Sept. 9.—To the Kremlin, seeing the Treasury, containing the various arms of the different reigns, the saddles, bridles, stirrups, swords, etc., being studded with precious stones—diamonds, rubies, turquoises, emeralds, sapphires, etc. Also the thrones—ivory, gold, and silver, encrusted with diamonds and rubies and immense turquoises. The collection of plate, in size, quantity, and shape, passes belief. In one room is the collection of crowns; that of Alexwitch has 881 diamonds, and under the cross an immense ruby. The crown of Peter the Great has 847 diamonds; that of Catharine I., 2,536—splendid stones, to which the Empress Anne added the largest ruby in the world. The throne of Michael Romanoff has 8,824 fine turquoises, many as large as a ten-cent piece, and 1,220 other jewels. After lunch, drive to Sparrow Hill, about 4 miles, where Napoleon, on the 14th of September, 1814, had his first view of Moscow. The

Opera-House is very superb, with the widest stage and largest orchestra in Europe.

Sept. 10.—To the Romanoff Palace, very small, but very characteristic of the early life of the present royal family before coming to the throne. Also to St. Basil's Church, with 11 chapels above and 6 below. After lunch, to the Foundling Hospital, the most wonderful institution of the sort in the world. Its revenues are 600 to 700 millions of rubles—more than twice the revenue of Prussia; having 10 per cent. on all the receipts of the theatres, and the monopoly of cards throughout the empire. Since 1st January last (hardly nine months), 7,890 children have been admitted, and 580,000 since its commencement; 25 children daily is the average number left here. The children are all educated to speak four languages; and, if they show ability, become tutors, governesses, music-teachers, etc.

Sept. 12.—Leaving Moscow in train at 1.30, reach St. Petersburg at 10 next morning.

Sept. 13.—See the École des Mines, filled with patterns and models of all the mines in Switzerland, Siberia, etc.; also the Winter Palace, with many pictures of great Russian battles; also the crown jewels, more magnificent than can well be described—one necklace, with diamonds each as large as a shilling. The throne-room, St. George's Hall, and other halls, superb; 7,000 persons reside here when the emperor comes to town for the season. In this palace is also to be seen the simple, unostentatious little chamber where the Emperor Nicholas died.

Sept. 14.—To the Hermitage, which really requires a week to be seen thoroughly. The magnificent collection of pictures being almost unsurpassed in any other gallery — Rubens, Vandyck, Guido, Teniers, etc., a room of each. The works of art, especially marbles, most superb. Exquisite vases, candelabras, tables of malachite, vert-antique, lapis-lazuli, pink and variegated marbles. The collection of antique rings very interesting. Afternoon, drive to the great palm-houses and botanic gardens belonging to the Czar (on the Apothecary's Island), who pays $45,000 a year for their support. There are 12 houses, very old and shabby, having been built over 30 years; the plants are very fine and large, the varieties of evergreens being over 3,000, two *araucarias*, over 35 feet high, costing $1,400.

Sept. 16.—By rail to Tzarko Selo, thence by carriage to the palace, the summer residence of the emperor, 14 versts from St. Petersburg; a splendid and curious old palace. The grounds, roads, arrangement of ornamental water, quite English in their character and keeping. Also drive to Paulovsky, the palace of the Grand-duke Michael. Back to St. Petersburg by 5.

Sept. 18.—To the Hermitage again, seeing the splendid collection of snuff-boxes and objects of Peter the Great, as well as the tools, turning-lathes, and various things made by him; also again revisit the magnificent gallery, especially the Russian Rubens and Vandyck rooms, as well as the Mæris, Van Steen, and Teniers collection. Later drive to the Taurida Palace, with its great ballroom, half a mile in circumference, and really beautiful gardens.

Sept. 22.—Leave St. Petersburg in a *cabinet particulier* (carriage on rail), at 1, and, after travelling all night, breakfast next morning at the station in Wilna, lunching at another station at 2, and reaching Warsaw (Hôtel de l'Europe), at 6 P. M., after 30 hours in train.

Sept. 23.—Taking a carriage, drive round the town, seeing the palaces of the old Polish nobles—the Sobieskis, Poniatowskis, Bruhls, etc.; and out to the summer palace of the emperor, built by the last Polish king—certainly the most charming house, water, and grounds, ever imagined. Just beyond, the Belvidere, the palace of the Grand-duke Constantine.

Sept. 25.—Leave Warsaw at 1, by train, changing cars at Bromberg; at Thorn passing the Russian, and at Alexandravitch the Prussian, frontier, and reaching Berlin at 6 the next morning (Hotel St. Petersburg).

Oct. 2.—Leave Berlin at 6 A. M. by train; reach Cologne at 9.30 P. M.; 403 English miles.

Oct. 4.—Leave Cologne (Bellevue Hotel), at 9 A. M., by train; reaching Brussels at 3.30 (Bellevue, a most excellent hotel).

Oct. 10.—Leave Brussels by express train, at 9.05; reaching Paris (Hôtel Bristol) at 5 P. M.

NOTE.—The entire journey from London, back to Paris, including Belgium, Holland, Hanover, Denmark, Norway, Sweden, Russia, Poland, Prussia, occupied 4 months and 4 days, and might readily have been accomplished in 3 months. The entire cost 19,446 francs—say 4,000 dollars in gold—for actual travelling expenses; and for a party of 4 and 1 servant, and in Norway 2 servants.

TOURS THROUGH SICILY AND SPAIN.

PARIS TO MALTA, MALTA VIA SICILY, NAPLES, ROME, FLORENCE, GENOA, THE CORNICHE ROAD, AND SPAIN TO PARIS.

Jan. 1.—Leaving Paris at 7 P. M. by train (*coupé au lit*), reach Marseilles next day at noon (Grand Hôtel de Marseilles).

Jan. 3.—Leaving Marseilles at 8 A. M. in steamer, reach Malta third afternoon at 6 P. M. (Dunsford's Hotel).

Feb. 20.—Leaving Malta at 5 P. M., reach Syracuse in Sicily at 4 next morning. Quitting steamer after breakfast, visit the fountains of Arethusa, the museum, the Temples of Minerva and Ceres, the Ear of Dionysius, etc., returning to steamer at 11. Reach Catania (Grand Hotel) at 2; beautifully situated. Leave steamer here.

Feb. 21.—See the town and the grand street Victor Emmanuel; by carriage to the magnificent church of the Benedictines, the largest in Sicily; then to the remains of the Greek Theatre, built before Christ, said to hold 3,000 persons—the amphitheatre of seats and much of the exquisite carved marble in the finest preservation. After this, to a pretty public garden, with araucarias, palms, aloes, etc., the banks being masses of verbenas, petunias, lobelias, to cover the naked ground, instead of grass. In the Botanic Garden are beautiful specimens of araucaria-bidwillii, biota-canariensis, taxodium-mucronatum, and casurina-torulosa.

Feb. 22.—If clear, the finest view of Mount Etna is from the hotel. Leave Catania by train at 3, reaching Messina at 6.40, over a most superb road and through interesting scenery; many towns on top of mountains, and picturesque old castles. At Messina, Hotel Victoria excellent.

Feb. 23.—Walk about the town and up the Strada Victor Emmanuel to the Catania Gate. In the afternoon drive to a beautiful view over the city.

Feb. 24.—Leave Messina at 8 A. M. in steamer, passing through Scylla and Charybdis, just outside the straits, and by Stromboli, wreathed in volcanic smoke, about 10. At 12 reach Lipari, a picturesque town on top of a mountain, where the boat stops an hour. This is on one of the Æolian isles. At 4 reach Molasso, remaining here four hours, and arriving at Palermo at noon the next day (The Trinacria); excellent hotel. The passage from Messina to Palermo should, if possible, be always taken by daylight, as it is inexpressibly charming; the most extraordinary towns, convents, and castles, perched up on top of apparently inaccessible mountains—many in ruins. Palermo itself hardly inferior in situation to Naples.

Feb. 25.—Walk to the English Garden (beautifully situated on the Marina), and to the elaborate Moorish cathedral; drive to Baida, a deserted monastery, superbly situated on a mountain, with magnificent views of Palermo; from here to the gardens of the Duke of Ragusa, with a well-contrived labyrinth and rustic house, on opening the doors of which, a monk rushes at you from one and blesses you from another. The place itself a tangled mass of exquisite exotics (all the varieties of palms, yuccas, aloes, araucarias, acacias, casuarinas 20 feet high, india-rubber as large as apple-trees, abutilons, daphnes, evergreens), magnolias, etc., and camphor-trees, through which run walks in every direction.

Feb. 26.—Leaving the hotel at 10 A. M., drive in carriage to Monte Reale, a superb old convent on top of a mountain 5 miles from Palermo, with a wonderful view of the city, sea, and valley; connected with it is a church, perfectly encrusted and lined with mosaics—one piece of floor lately repaired, some 20 × 50 feet, cost £4,000. The cloisters here are also very beautiful, each column and capital being of different design. The view from the terrace of Monte Reale is perhaps as fine as any thing in Europe. Visit on your way back the Capuchin convent, containing 8,000 dried monks—one who died in 1600 having his nails, fingers, and tongue, quite perfect.

Feb. 27.—Drive in one and a half hours to Bacheria, seeing the wonderful palace of the monsters; the avenues having, at intervals, on parapets and pedestals, the most grotesque figures in stone, of devils, demons, etc.; the interior very magnificent, though in decay; the grand drawing-room, 60 feet square, being ceiled in mirrors, on which were painted various figures; the walls of different-colored porphyry and marbles, with busts and figures of the family in *alto relievo;* the floor of marble, alabaster, and porphyry. Another palace hard by, belonging to Prince Riso, had a terrace from which were exquisite views of Palermo and its bay, and a second bay on the other side of the mountains. The palace of Prince Bouterer also very interesting, with superb views, and having near it a house filled with wax-figures of priests in their different occupations, very well done. Back to Palermo at 5.

Feb. 28.—Leaving Palermo at 1 in steamer, reach Naples next morning at 6 (The Victoria Hotel).

March 6.—Leaving Naples by rail at 10.30, reach Rome (Hôtel de Rome) at 7 P. M.

March 16.—Leaving Rome at 8 P. M. by train (*coupé au lit*), reach Florence next morning to breakfast (Hôtel de l'Arno).

March 22.—Leaving Florence by rail at 10.45 A. M., reach Pisa at 1.15. Leaving Pisa by a later train at 3.30, reach Genoa at 4. After dinner at the hotel, take steamer at 8 P. M., arriving at Genoa (Hôtel Feder) at 5.30 next morning. After seeing the town, drive a few miles to the Villa Pallavicini, not usually visited by travellers, but more remarkable than any gardens in Italy, or possibly in the world. The estate is kept in order by 20 directors, 8 gardeners, and 30 assistants, the usual pay being 2 to 3 francs a day: you pass from the house on to a superb terrace of white marble, having a very extended view over the city and the Mediterranean, as far as the mountains of Corsica; below, a series of terraces, with white-marble balustrades and steps—these terraces bordered by espaliers of oranges and lemons, 20 feet high, and standard camellias (10 to 20 feet high) of every color, in full flower; these were interspersed with large azalias and rhododendrons, also in bloom. From the other side of the house you enter (through avenues of laurel and laurestinus, heath in flower 12 to 15 feet high, 8 or 10 varieties of holly) the beautiful Grecian temple in white marble, with exquisite frescos. On the other side of this is a long Italian walk, bordered by vases, and planted with dwarf oranges in fruit, with a background of firs, and terminating in another beautiful temple. From this again you pass through narrow, tortuous walks, to a little rustic cottage, designed to show the contrast between high art and simple Nature. Ascending through dense woods of holly, laurel, Portugal laurel, and sweet bay, surmounted by majestic Italian pines, you come suddenly upon a wild, picturesque fall, the water brought 5 miles, forming a small lake, in which the fish are fed at a cost of $2.50 a day. This walk, with occasional stopping-places, indicated by rustic seats, leads to the summit of the mountain, upon which is a ruined tower, with superb views in every direction. Descending the mountain through similar plantations, you come, amidst dense undergrowth of yew and holly, upon some ruins, intended to represent a city destroyed by war—mossy and ivy-grown. A turn in the walk suddenly brings you in front of a cavern of stalactites, brought at great expense from every part of Italy; you pass through intense gloom and shadow for some way, presently emerging into a lighter cavern, 80 feet square, the crevices of the rocks overgrown and draped with ivy and parasites, admitting sufficient daylight to perceive a large lake, occasionally appearing and disappearing between the columns and walls of the cavern. Your guide now saluting you, says, "Addio, signor! I shall again behold you in the Temple of Flora!" and suddenly leaves you. Presently, in the dim, distant windings of this mysterious cavern, a gilded boat appears, propelled by a picturesque Charon; you enter, and, after several minutes of alternate light and shade, passing through narrow, gloomy passages, where the dimmest light is only seen, and again into large caverns—luminous through crevices in vaulted roofs of rock,—you suddenly emerge into the bright sun in a beautiful little lake. In the centre is an island, on which stands a most charming and exquisitely-sculptured temple, containing a statue of Diana; at some little distance, in the water, are four statues of the Tritons. There are several other small islands, connected by Chinese bridges, elaborate in color and gold; under one you have, from your boat, a most exquisite view of the Mediterranean, some 700 feet below. On another side of this little lake is a charming garden, surrounded by dense, umbrageous plantations of arbutus, oleander, and laurestinus, containing a parterre exquisitely laid out and planted in azalias and camellias, of every shade of color: in the midst stands a lovely little temple of purest marble, called the Temple of Flora. Here you disembark, and are again received by your former guide, who informs you that this grotto and lake cost nine hundred thousand francs, and occupied four hundred men daily for two years to complete it. Passing a cork-tree, said to be the largest in Italy, you come to a rustic bridge leading to a summer-house, beyond which is a swing. On crossing the bridge, a loose plank touching a spring covers you with water; running into the rustic-house to get rid of this, you find yourself the centre of four horizontal sheets of water. If you attempt the swing, you are drenched from all the adjacent trees. Return to Genoa at 6.

March 25.—Leave Genoa at 10 A. M., with vetturino and four horses, who, for ten napoleons, delivers you at Nice. You stop at Cagoletto, the birthplace of Columbus, to lunch, reaching Savonna to dine and sleep about 6.

March 26.—Leave Savonna at 8.30; reach Oneglia at 5.30 to dine and sleep.

March 27.—Leave Oneglia at 9; reach Mentone at 5 to dine and sleep.

March 28.—Leave Mentone at 8.30, arriving at Nice at 1.30, and, taking rail at 3.20, reach Marseilles at 9.05 P. M. (Grand Hotel).

NOTE.—As the intention of these routes is simply to be a guide through those countries and places not so well known as others, all details of what to see in Naples, Rome, Florence, Genoa, etc. (with the exception of the account of the Pallavicini Gardens), have been omitted here. In fact, upon this journey the writer merely passed through these cities, having made long visits to them in previous years.

March 31.—Leave Marseilles at 11.30, reaching Nismes at 2.25. See the beautiful Maison Carrée, the Amphitheatre, and the exquisite Jardin de la Fontaine, with superb fountain and Temple of Diana, etc., after lunch. Leave Nîsmes at 5; reaching Montpellier (Hôtel Nevet) at 6.50.

April 1.—Visit the celebrated Jardin Peyrou, quite the finest in Europe, the water-tower most exquisite, and the equestrian statue of Louis XIV. as fine as that of Marcus Aurelius at Rome. The Botanic Garden, founded by Henry V., in 1598, very interesting, especially a *Cupressus pendula* from Japan, and an avenue of clipped Judas-trees. The old Moorish porch of the cathedral, as well as the new Palais de Justice, are very fine. The Musée of Pictures, especially the smaller room, one of the most interesting galleries in the world; containing 11 Greusés and 11 Teniers, all in exquisite order. Leave Montpellier by train at 12.50, reaching Cette in 30 minutes; lunching at an excellent *buffet*. On again by rail at 3, reaching Perpignan at 6.50, where sup. Taking the first Spanish diligence at 10, and driving all night, reaching the Spanish frontier at 3 A. M., where luggage is examined. At 10, reach Geroma, to breakfast, and at 12, taking a train, reach Barcelona (Hôtel de 4 Naciones) at 3.35.

April 2.—Visit the cathedral, where the instalment of the Knights of the Golden Fleece took place; very handsome, especially the stained glass, said to be the finest in Spain; the churches, Santa Maria del Mar and Santa Maria del Pino, Casa de la Disputacion, with some fine old Moorish arches. Drive to the Rambla in the evening.

April 3.—Leave Barcelona at 8 o'clock (Madrid time), reaching Tarragona at 11.30, a very ancient and Spanish-looking city (Hôtel Fonda de Paris.) Visit the cathedral, the altar being exquisitely finished, as well as the cloisters, said to be the finest in Spain; all the columns being different; one representing in its carving a cat pursuing some mice—the cat at one portion pretending to be dead, is carried off by the mice to be buried, but, presently awakening, attacks the mice right and left.

April 4.—Leave Tarragona at 8, by rail for two hours, and by diligence, drawn by six mules, for three hours, passing Tortosa, an ancient Spanish town. Taking a train about 3, reach Valencia (Fonda del Cid), at 9.30; passing through a country cultivated like a garden.

April 5.—Drive to the old Moorish palace, now the silk-mart, very characteristic and interesting. In the afternoon to the Glorieta, a beautiful drive, with a charming garden, planted with trimmed box, with standard orange-trees in full blossom; the flower-beds gay with tulips and all the early summer flowers.

April 6.—Ascend the cathedral, with the finest view in Spain, 260 steps to the top. Taking train at 2.10, reach Alicante at 9.50 (Fonda del Vapor).

April 7.—Drive in carriage 4 leagues (2 hours) to the Arab town of Elche, situated in an oasis of palms, most Oriental and Asiatic in appearance, from the palms and character of the Bedouin-like houses. In the Church of St. Maria is a statue of a virgin, which is held in great reputation—often dressed in expensive garments and jewels, etc. She is even a landed proprietor, having in her possession the finest palms and orchards, called "Huertos de la Virgen"—the produce goes to pay for her dresses, candles, and the expenses of the priests who have her in charge. The view from the tower, over this oasis of palms, is very striking.

April 8.—Leave Valencia in steamer at 10 P. M.; passing the next day, at a distance, Carthagena and other towns on the coast, and reaching Malaga at 3 on morning of the 10th of April (Hôtel Victoria).

April 10.—Drive a few miles, to a charming country-place belonging to Mr. Loring, now Marquis of Caridad, formerly of Boston. The garden beautifully arranged and planted—*araucarias*, palms, deodars, etc., only 11 years old, immense for their age.

April 11.—Leave Malaga in steamer at 6 A. M. After a very delightful passage along the coast of Spain, reach Gibraltar at 4.30 P. M.

April 12.—See the town. Walk through the galleries in the rock—most extraordinary—1,400 feet in height—guns in every direction—700 in all—6,000 men in garrison, provisioned for 7 years. It is supposed that it is impossible to take Gibraltar, but not impossible for a fleet to run through the straits, only 12 miles wide. In the evening in carriage to Europa Point, a most exquisite drive, not only from the views, but the beautiful plants and gardens on the road—the houses with pretty English-cottage effect, geraniums growing wild, and aloes flowering in abundance.

April 13.—Leave Gibraltar in steamer at 7 A. M., and after another charming voyage by the coast, reach Cadiz at 4 P. M.; beautifully situated on a peninsula. The houses all whitewashed, with green and blue verandas. The cleanest city in Spain. (Hotel, Fonda de Paris.)

NOTE.—From Gibraltar a very pleasant excursion may be made in two or three hours, across the straits, to Tangier, in Africa; returning next day to Gibraltar.

April 14.—Leave Cadiz at 6 A. M., passing Xeres at 8 (where you may stop for a later train), and reach Seville at 10.15 (Fonda de Paris).

April 15.—Visit House of Pontius Pilate, supposed to be a copy of the original house at Jerusalem—thoroughly Moorish and Alhambra-like in character, and very beautiful. Afterward to the Musée, to see the Murillos, of which the "St. Thomas giving Alms" is considered the finest; later to the cathedral, by many considered even more interesting than St. Peter's, the stained glass being very beautiful, and the carvings to the two organs most superb.

April 16.—To the Church of La Caridad, where are four more Murillos; "Moses striking Water from the Rock" and "The Miracle of the Loaves and Fishes" being considered the finest. After this to the wonderful Alcazar, the old palace of the Moorish kings, more perfect in color and restoration than can be easily imagined.

April 17.—Some of the festivities of Holy Week, as well as the bull-fights, usually commence about this time, and are well worth seeing; the display during Holy Week being even greater than at Rome—in fact, they are of sufficient importance to make it an object to the traveller to visit Seville during this period, though it is apt to be very crowded.

April 23.—Leave Seville by train at 10 A. M., reaching Cordova at 1.30 (Fonda Suisse). After lunch, visit the cathedral, the purest and best specimen of Moorish architecture in Spain; nearly 1,000 columns, most superb Moorish arches, with gilded and colored embroidery in plaster.

April 24.—Again visit the cathedral, also to "The View," with the old Moorish mill, Roman gates, and Spanish bridge. Taking train at 12, reach Malaga at 6.30 P. M. (Hôtel Victoria).

April 26.—Leave Malaga in diligence and four mules at 7 A. M., toiling up the mountains for five hours; wonderful views, with the wildest and most dreary scenery; an elevation of 3,000 feet above Malaga; reaching Loja to dine and sleep—an old Spanish *posada*, exactly as it was forty years ago, when Mr. Irving slept here, and described it.

April 27.—Leaving Loja at 4 A. M. by diligence for railway station, and by train at 5, reach Granada at 8.30, and the Hôtel Washington Irving (at the Alhambra) at 9, to breakfast. Make your first visit to the Alhambra; more perfect, delicate, and in better taste, than the Alcazar at Seville, though very much resembling it, but not so brilliant in colors; see the various towers, gardens, and grand views of the Vega and the Sierra Nevada.

NOTE.—The rail being probably now finished (1869), it will not be necessary, in coming from Cordova, to go entirely through to Malaga in order to get to Granada; but one can leave the Cordova and Malaga rail at a point opposite Loja, and thus go entirely through to Granada by rail.

April 28.—To the Alhambra in the morning, and afterward to the Certuja, founded by Bruno, with wonderfully rich marbles from the Sierra Nevada, and mosaic tables.

April 29.—To the Alhambra in the morning; later to the Gardens of the Generallif, the old summer-palace of the caliphs, beautifully kept up, and the trees (cypress) very curiously trained; charming roses and beautiful streams of water in every direction. In the palace is a very attractive portrait of Boabdil, the last Moorish king, with a mild and pleasant face, and also of all the Moorish and Christian kings and queens.

April 30.—To the royal chapel in the town of Granada, seeing the beautiful tombs of Ferdinand and Isabella, also of Philip le Bel and Crazy Jane, his wife, as well as the sword, crown, and sceptre, of Isabella. In the afternoon drive to the spot where Isabella erected a church in commemoration of her escape from the Moors on the capture of Granada, by concealing herself in a laurel-bush, which still exists. In evening visit at the Alhambra, the towers of the Captive Princess, and the three Princesses Zaida, Zoraida, and Zoraihaida, so beautifully told by Washington Irving; also the Mosquita, a little imitation of a Moorish mosque, built by a Spanish colonel.

May 3.—Leaving the Alhambra at 4 A. M. by carriage for the town below, take the diligence and 10 mules, breakfasting at 10 A. M. in a curious old *posada* at Jaen, and arriving at Menzibar at 4.30 P. M. Here dine at station, and, taking rail at 6 P. M., reach Madrid next morning at 6.30 (Fonda de Paris).

May 4.—Drive round the town and to the magnificent museum of pictures, wonderful in its collection of Murillos and Velasquez; also to the Armeria, seeing the splendid collection of armor and arms. In the afternoon, drive in the Prado.

May 5.—To the Gallery; later, palace and stables, containing 150 splendid horses—some magnificent Andalusians; hot and cold baths for the horses. In the carriage-houses are nearly 100 carriages, of different styles. In the afternoon to Toledo, returning to Madrid next day.

May 6.—Taking train at 8.30, reach the famous Escurial at 10.30. This wonderful combination of palace and mausoleum, built by Philip II. in 1567 (the resting-place of himself, as well as that of his father, Charles V.), cost, it is said, £800,000; contains 16 courts, 40 altars, 1,111 windows inside and 1,560 outside, 12,000 doors, 15 cloisters, 86 staircases, 3,000 feet of fresco, 89 fountains, and 32 leagues (160 miles) of surface. Nothing can well be more severe or gloomy, especially the little dark cell opening into the church, where Philip died. A portion of the palace, sometimes used by the present queen (since driven from the kingdom), is lovely—the walls, doors, and ceilings, exquisitely inlaid in marquetrie; the tapestry also very wonderful, many of the designs by Teniers being still perfectly fresh. The Casa del Principe is also a charming little palace, the walls and ceilings being exquisitely decorated. Return to Madrid at 8.30 P. M.

May 11.—Leave Madrid by train at 3.30, reaching Biarritz at noon next day (Hôtel de France).

May 13.—Leave Biarritz at 12, reaching Bordeaux (Hôtel de France) at 5.30.

May 15.—Leave Bordeaux at 9.30 by rail, reaching Tours (Hôtel de l'Universe) at 5. Beautiful excursions may be made from Tours to the great chateaux of Ambroise, Blois, Chaumont, Chambord, etc., etc.

May 17.—Leave Tours at 11.30 by rail, reaching Paris (Hôtel Bristol) at 4.40.

NOTE.—The journey from Malta through Sicily and Spain occupied about three months; the actual journey through Spain a little over six weeks, at a cost, for four persons and one servant, of eight thousand francs—say sixteen hundred dollars in gold.

THE END.

www.ingramcontent.com/pod-product-compliance
Lightning Source LLC
Chambersburg PA
CBHW020145170426
43199CB00010B/899